fresh start, feel good!

FRESH START
& NADIA LIM

Photography by Todd Eyre

CONTENTS.

say hello to your fresh start

If you've been wanting to lose some weight or just kickstart your health goals in an enjoyable, delicious and sustainable way (that'll keep the weight off!), then this book is for you.

Fresh Start, Feel Good! is the sequel to my *Fresh Start* cookbook. There was such an amazing response to that book (thank you to all those with a copy!), with people loving its realistic, down-to-earth recommendations and easy, delicious recipes. I'm proud to say that it has helped thousands of Kiwis to lose weight and keep it off, or just given them a better lease on their health and life, all while enjoying what they're eating and not having to follow any fads or inflexible diet rules or advice. Thank you to all who have sent me messages and shared your stories over the last few years – I love hearing them!

This book is also an extension of My Food Bag's Fresh Start, which delivers simple, healthy and delicious ingredients and recipes that are perfectly portioned and under 450 calories to help with weight maintenance or weight loss. So many of you were asking for a service that helped with the eating part of your journey that we just had to create a specialised weight-loss bag. Since its launch in 2017, it has helped thousands of customers not only lose weight but increase their energy levels, manage their diabetes, lower their blood pressure... the list goes on. It has been truly amazing and a privilege to be part of something that has changed so many people's lives for the better.

However, a lot of confusion around weight loss remains; there's no shortage of new diets, products and theories. In my time working as a dietitian (specialising in weight loss and diabetes), I realised just how confusing it can be to navigate the world of health and weight loss. What I can tell you is this: the only tried-and-true way that continuously works, without fail, is really quite simple – and it doesn't require any special ingredients, strict diet rules, becoming a label-reading expert or racking up an expensive grocery bill.

Healthy and delicious ingredients and recipes that are perfectly portioned and under 450 calories to help with weight maintenance or weight loss.

The Fresh Start team and I are 'Nude Food' advocates. We believe in getting back to basics, a way of eating that:

· ignores fads, diets and marketing hype (which just confuses people);

· focuses on and is about real food (food that's minimally processed and mostly comes from the ground, the sea and the sky) and eating less food processed in factories;

· involves listening to your body, because it knows better than anyone else and there is no one diet that fits all (we're far too genetically varied for that!).

Along with that, we're big believers that the only way something is going to work is if you enjoy the process as much as the result. How can you keep something up if you hate doing it? It won't last; it won't be sustainable. And that's why diets fail. People lose weight initially, only to put it back on when they can't keep up the unrealistic expectations that don't fit in with their lifestyles, genetics or taste buds. Flexibility and enjoyment are key.

And that's where our love and talent for finding the perfect balance between delicious-tasting food that is also good for you comes in. We like to pack in more nutrition and load up the fresh produce wherever we can – more vegetables, more fibre, more nourishing ingredients. To help with weight loss, all of our recipes are 450 calories or less per portion and they are also lower in carbohydrates and free of refined sugar (more on this later).

Anyway, enough 'talk'; let's get on with it and say hello to your Fresh Start!

Nadia x

Nadia and the Fresh Start team x

P.S. If you're looking for a break from food shopping and meal planning, you can get all the ingredients and recipes similar to those in this book from Fresh Start – check out myfoodbag.co.nz and let us do all the work for you!

lose weight

not flavour

Choose any breakfast, lunch, dinner (and snacks and dessert) to make up your own 1,200–1,600 calorie per day eating plan for 12 weeks, which will get results.

- Choosing three meals a day from this book will help you meet an average of 1,200 calories per day. Add on 1 or 2 snacks per day (including 1 fruit), and up to 1 sweet treat and 2 extras/treats per week, and that'll meet an average of 1,400–1,500 calories per day.

- This level of calorie intake, along with some moderate exercise, will see you lose weight. For most people, a good rate of weight loss is somewhere between 0.5–1kg per week. This is a level that is safe, realistic and sustainable. Remember, slow and steady wins the race!

- If you need more calories because you're not wanting to lose weight, you're male or you are more active than the average person, add on another snack per day and you can have a couple more extras over the week. Or simply slightly increase your portion size.

- On some days, you might want to make up your own meal – go for it! Check out the Food Groups and, as long as you substitute an equal quantity from each of the food groups listed, you can make up your own meal and still stick within the 12-week plan no problem!

1,200 calories per day	1,400–1,500 calories per day	1,600 calories per day
Breakfast	Breakfast	Breakfast
Lunch	Lunch	Lunch
Dinner	Dinner	Dinner
	Snacks (1–2 per day)	Snacks (2–3 per day)
	Dessert (up to 1 per week)	Dessert (up to 2 per week)
	Extras (up to 2 per week)	Extras (up to 3 per week)

Remember that it all starts with nutrition first and foremost, so to ensure you get loads of goodness from what you eat, you need to eat a variety and balance of the different food groups (because they are all stars in their own right when it comes to different nutrients!).

Carbs

Opt for minimally processed carbs such as kumara, or other starchy root vegetables, quinoa, legumes, etc., most of the time.

About 3 portions per day.

1 portion is equal to approximately:
— ½ cup cooked quinoa
— ½ cup cooked brown rice (or other rice)
— ½ cup cooked kumara or other starchy root vegetable
— ¾ cup cooked legumes (e.g. beans, chickpeas, lentils, etc.)
— 1 thin slice grainy bread or seed loaf
— 2 wholegrain crackers
— About ½ cup muesli or granola
— ⅓ cup oats

Vegetables

Non-starchy (non-carby) vegetables are the one food group that you can eat as much as you like – the more the better!

Eat at least 4–5 portions per day.

1 portion is equal to approximately:
— ¾–1 cup cooked or raw vegetables
— 1 big handful leafy greens

Fruit

Great as snacks, eat a wide variety.

About 2 portions per day.

1 portion is equal to approximately:
— What fits snugly in the palm of your hand, e.g. 2 small apricots or feijoas, 1 small apple or ½ large apple, 1 orange, ½ banana, 1 small pear
— ½ cup frozen fruit, e.g. berries or diced mango
— ½ cup canned (and well drained) fruit, e.g. peaches

Lean protein

About 2 portions per day.

1 portion is equal to approximately:
— 125–150g raw meat, fish, salmon or chicken
— 100g cooked meat, chicken or fish (including smoked)
— 2 eggs
— 100g tofu
— 1 cup cooked beans, lentils or chickpeas

Healthy fats

About 3 portions per day.

1 portion is equal to approximately:
— ¼ avocado
— 20g (1½ tablespoons) nuts and/or seeds
— 1 tablespoon oil (e.g. olive oil, avocado oil, coconut oil) or butter or substitute
— 2 tablespoons nut or seed butter (e.g. cashew nut or peanut butter)

Dairy and substitutes

About 2 portions per day.

1 portion is equal to approximately:
— 1 cup milk of any kind, e.g. almond, cow's, soy, oat or rice milk
— ½ cup yoghurt
— 20–25g full-fat cheese, such as Parmesan or cheddar
— 50–75g lower fat cheese, such as feta, halloumi or mozzarella

Drinks

— No more than 1 cup of coffee per day
— To limit caffeine intake, we suggest no more than 3 cups of black tea per day
— At least 8 glasses of water per day
— You can also drink as much herbal tea as you like
— Alcohol comes under Treats and Extras

Treats and extras

Up to 2–4 portions per week.

1 portion is equal to any extra food or drink that equates to around 100 calories (420kJ) such as:
— 1 x 130ml glass of wine or 250ml beer
— 1 small 200ml hot chocolate
— 20g (4 squares) chocolate

	Recipe	Food groups
Breakfast	Pesto Eggs on Roast Mushrooms, Cherry Tomatoes and Spinach (p.57)	1 portion lean protein 2–3 portions vegetables 1½ portions healthy fats
Lunch	Brown Rice Veggie Bowl with Smoked Salmon, Sesame and Pickled Ginger (p.97)	1 portion carbohydrate 1 portion lean protein 1 portion vegetables
Dinner	Parmesan-Crumbed Chicken with Balsamic and Honey Roasted Veg (p.144)	1 portion lean protein 2–3 portions vegetables ½ dairy
Snacks	Fro-yo (p.230) Avocado Hummus with Spinach, Lemon and Chilli (p.212)	1 snack (also provides 1½ portions fruit and ½ portion dairy/subs) 1 snack (also provides ½ portion healthy fat, ½ –1 portion vegetables, 1½ portions carbohydrate)
Sweet *(1 per week)*	Chocolate Custard with Orange and Cinnamon Prunes (p.278)	1 dessert (also provides 1 portion fruit and 1 portion dairy/subs)
Extras *(up to 2 per week)*	20g/4 squares dark chocolate	1 extra
Drinks	6 glasses water 3 herbal teas 1 small cup coffee	9 cups fluid (coffee not counted)

DAY	Breakfast	Lunch	Dinner	Snacks	Sweet/extras
1	Chewy No-grainola (p.54)	Butter Chicken Soup (p.77)	Lime and Chilli Glazed Fish with Edamame, Radish Salad and Brown Rice (p.143)	Yoghurt Bran Fruit Muffin (p.227) 1 small apple with nut butter	
2	Rosemary, Ham and Parmesan Scramble (p.65)	Chinese Chicken and Cabbage Salad (p.81)	Creamy Mushroom Steak with Root Veg Chips (p.180)	Roasted Cauliflower Hummus with Veggie Sticks and Crackers (p.213) ½ banana	
3	2 poached eggs on 1 slice of toast with spinach and tomato	Roast Veg and Quinoa Salad with Spiced Nuts and Feta (p.86)	Pumpkin, Chickpea and Courgette Curry, Brown Rice and Kachumber (p.148)	Roasted Cauliflower Hummus with Veggie Sticks and Crackers (p.213) 1 pear	
4	Chewy No-grainola (p.54)	Broccoli and Peanut Noodles with Sesame Avocado (p.74)	Moroccan Lamb Salad with Roast Carrots and Grape Bulghur (p.132)	Creamy Cauli, Berry and Banana Smoothie (p.205)	
5	Avocado on Toast (p.43)	Mediterranean Tuna and Chickpea Salad (p.98)	Chicken, Mango and Feta Pizza (p.176)	Chia Seed Pudding (p.199) Spicy Chilli and Cheese Popcorn (p.220)	Passionfruit Cheesecake Slice (p.291)
6	Pesto Eggs on Roast Mushrooms, Cherry Tomatoes and Spinach (p.57)	Butter Chicken Soup (p.77)	Hawaiian Grilled Chicken and Pineapple with Avocado in Lettuce 'Bun' (p.183)	Cucumber rounds with cottage cheese and smoked salmon	1 small glass wine
7	Broccoli, Capsicum and Feta Omelette (p.58)	You might decide to have lunch out!	Salmon and Lemony Greens with Pea Crush (p.151)		

FRESH
START
LOVE.

"

We've been doing this for about 4 weeks now. Cannot recommend highly enough. Easy, delicious and really satisfying. I love to cook and am pretty good at it, but find the meals interesting enough to cook with lots of different and exciting ingredients. Introduced both of us to new vege and ways to cook them. If you're looking to break old habits and not crave big carb-laden dinners, this is the way to do it. I think we'd both think twice now about eating a meal that wasn't chocka with veges. Really feel like refined sugar/flour addiction has been cracked and Fresh Start has helped so much.

Anna Connell

"

So far, 20 kg donated back to the universe that I don't need to lug around. Started early January. Thank you Nadia and Fresh Start for making it less painful and somewhat enjoyable whipping up your amazing recipes. As Dory says 'just keep swimming'.

Michelle Keen

"

I did it! I set myself a target and I did it. I have quite a bit to lose so I made a goal of 10 kg chunks a school term. I struggled a bit with a weekend away and Easter… Well it's the last day of term 1, I just weighed myself and lost 800 g this week to make it 10.5 kg total this term! Thanks Fresh Start!

Donna

"

I'm already halfway to my goal of losing 10 kg before my holiday in two months' time — so exciting! My husband is enjoying our meals and feeling a bit lighter too — bonus!

Alex Harms

"

I've been on the Fresh Start meals since they started and I've lost 12 kg. My husband had no idea we were eating fewer calories and is still quite bemused by the 4 kg that have mysteriously disappeared off his waistline.

Bernadette Wilson

"

I am one happy girl!! I set myself a goal in January to lose 10 kg by April and I smashed that goal, losing 14 kg instead. This means that I am almost halfway to my goal of 30 kg, but taking much less time than I thought it would! My mindset has changed so much that when I went to Hawaii recently I continued to make good decisions about my eating without missing out on too much and I only gained a measly 900 g. I am hugely grateful to Fresh Start and there is absolutely no way I would have been able to get here without it. I enjoy the variety of the yummy dishes and the Fresh Start community on Facebook; who would've thought you could be inspired and motivated by a group of people you don't know.

Kylie Clark

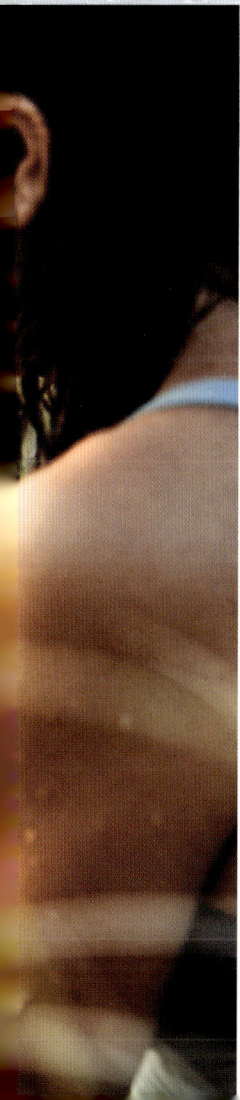

the a–z of being your best!

A

ABSORPTION.

You are what you absorb, even more than you are what you eat! Work on optimal digestion and absorption to ensure you're maximising the power of the nutrients in your food. You can have the best diet in the world, but if you don't absorb it then what's the point? Good absorption of nutrients starts with good digestion (see 'D' for Digestion) and a healthy, happy, well-functioning gut (see 'G' for Gut Health). Food allergies and intolerances can upset the absorption process, so if you have signs of IBS (Irritable Bowel Syndrome) involving problems with digestion, cramping, constipation, diarrhoea, bloating and gas, prioritise getting this sorted. IBS has become pretty common in our population. Food plays a major role; however, it is also believed that our more fast-paced, consistently stressful lives that result in constant adrenaline production are also to blame. The result is your body goes into 'fight or flight' mode, diverting blood flow away from what it considers to be non-important processes such as digestion to put into resources to 'save' your life.

Eating a wide, varied diet will also help maximise absorption because certain nutrients are better absorbed in the presence of others – for example, vitamin C helps increase the absorption of iron, and fat is needed for absorption of the fat-soluble vitamins A, D, E and K. Conversely, there are such things as anti-nutrients that compete with and decrease absorption of other important nutrients. Examples are phytates, oxalates and tannins – found in food/drink like tea, coffee, red wine, and raw legumes (cooked is fine), so avoid/reduce these as much as possible, especially around meal times to ensure they don't interfere with maximising your absorption of the good stuff!

B

BREAKFAST.

You might think that skipping breakfast is an easy way to lose weight, but it has the opposite effect! Not eating breakfast leads to binge eating later on. Countless studies show that it's the most important meal of the day, linked to successful weight loss and maintenance. Plus, what an opportunity to start the day off well! I love having a green smoothie every morning, along with a couple of eggs and some spinach and tomato. Before I've walked out the door, I've already had a couple of serves of veggies!

If you make it a habit to always start off with a nutritious breakfast, you don't have to worry so much if the day 'falls apart' and you end up making some not-so-nutritious choices. If you find it hard to stomach a meal first thing in the morning, no worries, just have something small and simple like a piece of fruit or a smoothie and have your breakfast a bit later on. If you often have to do a mad rush out the door, it's handy to have 'on-the-go' type breakfasts ready, like the Yoghurt Bran Fruit Muffins (page 227) or PB 'n' J Breakfast Jars (page 53). Alternatively, take something like the Chewy No-Grainola (page 54) and a pottle of yoghurt to work with you. There's never an excuse not to have a good brekkie!

B VITAMINS.

B vitamins convert nutrients from food into energy the body can use. There are 12 different B vitamins; however, thiamine, riboflavin and niacin are the ones primarily involved in energy metabolism. Luckily these B vitamins are widely distributed throughout our foods, so if you eat a varied diet it is likely that you're getting enough of these key micronutrients.

C

COUNT WHAT MATTERS.

It's not necessary to count calories, grams of fat, carbs or even the number on the bathroom scales too closely. If you're watching your weight and weighing yourself, try not to jump on the scales any more than once every 1 to 2 weeks. Instead, it's far more important (and useful long term) to shift your focus, attention and efforts to how well you're nourishing yourself. It's only once your body is in a relaxed, happy (well-nourished) state that it'll start to lose weight. So if you're going to count anything, count what matters most, i.e. the nutrients you're getting, by making nutritious food choices and ticking off all the food groups every day.

What is most important, above all, is how you feel – the positive reinforcement of feeling good, with more energy, is what will see you ultimately succeed in the long run.

CALORIES.

Note that while our recipes are 450 calories and under, we don't believe it's necessary to strictly count calories – what is way more important (and is going to help you most) is to focus on making sure you're super-nourished with all the goodness, energy, vitamins and minerals your body needs. Nutrition always comes first – only a well-nourished (happy) body will start to lose weight, whereas an undernourished body will crave more food in an attempt to get the nutrients it needs!

D

DIGESTION.

Good digestion starts with chewing your food well and eating slowly. Aim to eat your meal over at least 15–20 minutes (however, I now realise that this can be a bit of a challenge if you have little ones!). Chewing your food helps to mechanically break it down, making it easier to digest once it gets to your tummy, thus putting less strain on your digestive system. Also, the satiating hormone leptin (that triggers a feeling of fullness) takes 15–20 minutes to activate and signal to your brain that you've eaten enough, hence eating fast leads to over-eating.

If you've become a fast eater over the years, retrain yourself by putting your knife and fork down between every mouthful and counting at least 20 chews.

A little apple cider vinegar (ACV) or lemon juice in a small glass of warm water can also be helpful for stimulating stomach acid production to help break down and digest your food.

(VITAMIN) D.

Vitamin D is incredibly important for our immune system and mood. A significant number of us have below recommended levels for optimum health – a result of our changing lifestyle, where we spend more time indoors rather than out and about. Dietary sources of vitamin D are a bit limited, with main sources being oily fish, butter and egg yolks. However, the very best way to get your vitamin D is by safe sun exposure – getting outside and exposing your skin to 20 minutes' sunshine a day (depending on the time of year) will ensure you're good for this important vitamin.

DINING OUT.

Check out the menu online before going out to a restaurant so you know what options you have and you can plan ahead. Snack on vegetable sticks before you go out so you're not ravenous when you get there. Order an entrée and a side of vegetables or salad (instead of a main) if you're planning on having dessert, or even two entrées as your entrée and main.

If you forget to take a healthy lunch with you to work don't fret. There are still good choices you can make such as 5–6 pieces of regular sushi, a roast vegetable salad, clear chicken noodle soup, pumpkin soup or a pita pocket with protein and veggies.

E

ENERGY!

There are few people who'd say they don't want more energy! How do you maximise your energy levels through what you eat?
– Work on optimal digestion and absorption to ensure you're maximising the power of the nutrients in your food and getting all the energy you can from them.
– Apart from getting enough fuel from the macronutrients (carbs, fats and protein) that you eat, there are some key micronutrients you need to make sure that you're getting enough of. One of these is iron (see 'I' for Iron for more). B vitamins are also important (see 'B' for B vitamins).

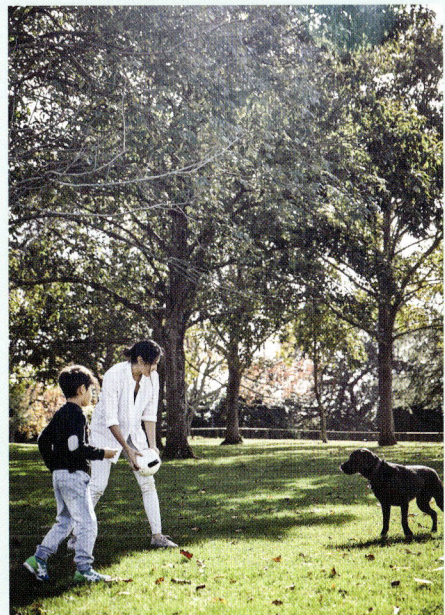

– It's common to feel like a nap or experience the 'post-meal slump', particularly after lunch time. The key to enjoying sustained energy from your food is in how that food releases its energy. Highly refined, high glycaemic (high GI) foods such as processed/refined carbs are digested very quickly, releasing glucose into your bloodstream quickly, eliciting a quick release of insulin from your pancreas (to use up the glucose and store it as fat). But what goes up, must come down, and this glucose spike results in a fast drop of blood glucose levels (the 'slump'). On the other hand, high-fibre foods, fat and protein take much longer for the body to break down, process and absorb, giving you a much more stable, consistent energy release. So make sure lunch is loaded with vegetables, and includes some fats and protein, and just a small amount of carbs (and make sure they're smart carbs that are minimally processed, low GI and fibre rich).

– Cutting down on caffeine and alcohol will also help improve your energy levels in the long run (see also 'Q' for Quit (or cut down on) Caffeine and Alcohol).

EXERCISE.

Motivation will get you started, but habit is what keeps you going. Research shows that it takes an average of 21 consecutive days of doing something for it to become a habit.

The aim is to do at least 30–45 minutes per day, on at least 5 days of the week. If it's a challenge to do your exercise all in one go, no sweat – just break it up into 15–20-minute chunks. A bit in the morning, some during your lunch break or after work is perfect.

You don't need to join a gym or buy any fancy exercise equipment to do effective exercise. Just Google body weight exercises and you'll find heaps of exercises you can do just using a chair or bench, the floor, and your own body weight!

For best results, you need both resistance (weight and/or body weight) training as well as cardio exercise. In a nutshell, resistance/weight training builds muscle, and more muscle mass means a faster metabolism. Cardio/aerobic exercise that gets your heart rate

going and makes you puff keeps you fit. Together they produce a much better metabolic response – after doing a resistance and cardio workout your metabolism can remain elevated for up to 18 hours!

Vary the type and intensity of exercise you do from day to day – a brisk 45-minute walk, a gentle jog, swimming, a fitness class, boot camp, dance class, resistance workout at home – there are endless things to do. Have 1 or 2 rest days per week; however, on these days you still need to be doing some moving, whether it's a leisurely walk on the weekend or a relaxing yoga class.

And don't forget about 'snacktivity' – wherever you can or see the opportunity to get a few extra minutes of movement/activity into your day, do it! Get in the habit of always opting to take the stairs, getting up to change the TV channel, parking a bit further away so you get a wee walk in – it all adds up and is a great habit to carry into your older years.

ENVIRONMENT.

Create a healthy environment by clearing out the pantry of any unhealthy temptations and make sure nutritious foods are plentiful in the fridge and fruit bowl: if something is readily available, and right in front of you, you'll be far more likely to eat it. Keep nutritious snacks in the freezer and make sure 'super foods' like leafy greens, berries, avocados and eggs are always on your shopping list. If you have some lean protein (ideally portioned out) in the fridge or freezer and fresh vegetables, there will always be a quick, healthy meal you can whip up, removing the risk of resorting to takeaways.

F

FAT.

Learn to love healthy fats! They're your (very good) friend. Including healthy fats (the mono- and poly-unsaturated kinds) in your diet does wonders for your health and vitality – everything from having great skin, to hormone levels, good cholesterol and satiety. Avocado, nuts and seeds, eggs, salmon and other oily fish, chia seeds, extra-virgin olive oil, avocado oil and coconut oil are all awesome. To keep all the recipes in this book under 450 calories we have limited the amount of oil used for cooking, but it's OK to use a little more (if needed) if you are not watching your weight too closely.

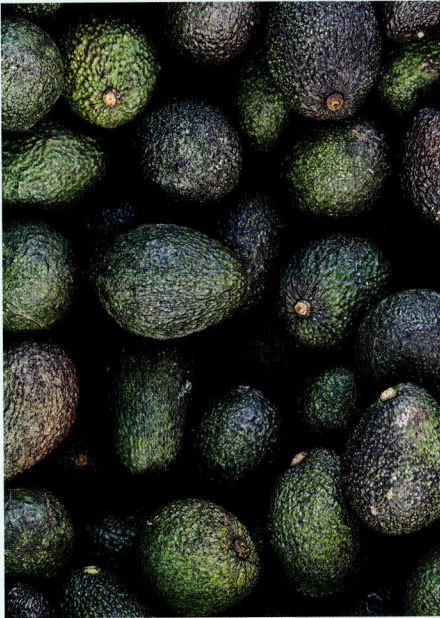

G

GUT HEALTH.

Your gut health and function is so important and in tune with how your mind and body feels that it is actually called the 'second brain'. The bacteria in your gut weighs up to 2kg alone. To ensure that you're looking after this happy, flourishing 'city' of living microorganisms eat lots of real food (and less processed foods), fibre and include lots of prebiotic foods that your healthy gut bacteria love and thrive on. When the good bugs in your gut are in the right balance, they aid digestion, helping to break down your food and eliminate waste.

Prebiotics are essentially the food/fuel that healthy gut bacteria just love. So the more prebiotics you eat, the more your healthy gut bacteria will thrive! Good sources of prebiotics include raw garlic, leek, onion, asparagus, banana, beans and legumes, bran, root vegetables and apples, and also fermented foods such as yoghurt, sauerkraut/kimchi, kombucha (make sure it is less than 2g sugar per 100ml), kefir, and tempeh (fermented tofu) which also contain lactobacillus cultures (which are termed probiotics – actual living microorganisms that are beneficial to our gut health). While you can take probiotic and prebiotic supplements for a boost, it's far better (and more effective) to prioritise getting it from your food.

With a healthy happy gut, and optimal digestion and absorption, you'll be maximising the power of the nutrients in your food. Remember, you are what you absorb, even more so than you are what you eat!

H

HYDRATE.

Drink plenty of water or other non-caffeinated, calorie-free drinks. A rough guide is 8 glasses per day. However, more importantly, pay attention to the colour of your pee – it should be a pale straw colour most of the time, which indicates you are drinking enough. (Note: If you're taking vitamin supplements your pee will be much brighter, but you can still determine whether or not it's light or too dark.) Many people need more than 8 glasses per day and it depends on how much you naturally sweat, talk, how active you are, etc.

It's easy to confuse hunger with thirst, so sometimes you can end up eating extra calories when a cold glass of water is all you really needed. If plain water doesn't cut it, have sparkling water with a squeeze of lime/lemon, or a cup of fruit-infused herbal tea (which is nice both hot or cold).

FIBRE.

Fibre keeps you regular, helps with weight loss and lowers cholesterol. Many people only get half their fibre requirements for the day. To ensure you're getting your fibre-fill, load up on vegetables, beans, legumes, fruit, nuts and seeds.

You need both soluble and insoluble fibre – both are equally important and play different roles in the gut. Insoluble fibre is what your mum or grandmother would have called 'roughage'; it promotes movement through your bowels, acting kind of like a 'scrubbing brush' to clear stuff out regularly. It's found in fruits and vegetables, particularly when you eat the skin, and nuts. Whereas soluble fibre, found in beans, peas, apples, pears, oats, bran, etc., dissolves when mixed with water and effectively acts like a 'sponge', soaking up water and swelling up, making your bowel contents softer and easier to move and pass. It's soluble fibre that is also beneficial for your cholesterol levels and can help with blood sugar management too.

While I believe that we can have everything in moderation, fizzy drinks are the one thing I suggest you eliminate entirely. They are so devoid of any nutrition and so intensely sweet that if you don't kick the habit you'll never get used to eating less sugar. While diet/artificially sweetened drinks contain next to no calories, they're still not recommended – drinking them will just keep you tuned to an unnaturally high level of sweetness, and on top of that there's a lot we don't know about these artificial additives and their long-term safety.

I

IMMUNITY.

Having a good immune system is so crucial for feeling your best. If you're constantly battling illness it's hard to put your resources towards exercising and eating well. Getting enough rest, good quality sleep, de-stressing and eating well are all essential for boosting your immune system. However, there are a few key nutrients that are especially important and play a significant role in immunity. These are zinc (see 'Z' for Zinc), vitamin D (see 'D' for vitamin D) and vitamin C (which you simply get from eating lots of fresh veg and fruit).

IRON.

Apart from getting enough fuel from the macronutrients (carbs, fats and protein) that you eat, there are some key micronutrients you need to make sure that you're getting enough of for great energy. One of these is iron. If you're experiencing severe fatigue, get your iron levels checked. You need adequate iron levels to carry enough oxygen in your blood to support processes in your cells. So if you're deficient in iron, it can feel like you're running a marathon every day. Sub-optimal iron levels are a common problem (especially in women) for various reasons from poor diet to pregnancy, childbirth and poor absorption.

J

JOY AND POSITIVITY.

The more you enjoy what you're doing, the more likely you are to stick with it. Encourage a friend or your partner to exercise with you or join a fitness group – having others in the same boat will encourage and motivate you more. Look after and reward yourself – your body is a temple and deserves treats (but non-food ones!), fun and R 'n' R. Surround yourself with positive vibes – even having an energising environment at home, with upbeat music and essential oils or candles, will make you feel more motivated and positive, and positive thinking has the power to change the course of your life.

K

BE KIND (AND LISTEN) TO YOUR BODY.

Work with your body, not against it, as it knows best what it needs. This means you need to eat when you're hungry (i.e. don't starve yourself), sleep when you're tired, and stop an exercise if it hurts. It's good to push yourself out of your comfort zone, but only in ways that are kind to your body and rejuvenate it to make it feel more energised.

L

LOVE REAL FOOD.

Real food – food from the ground, sea and sky, not the highly processed stuff in packets – is chock-full of useful nutrients. There's no need to decipher food labels or health claims when you stick to eating real, natural, unprocessed food, because it's all good for you! The high level of processing that many foods go through typically involves nutrients being stripped out and unhealthy fats, sugar, salt and preservatives being added to prolong shelf life. The end result is calories with no nutrition ('empty calories'), which will leave your body hungry for more food in an attempt to gain the nutrition it needs. On top of that, highly processed foods are 'dead' foods, i.e. they don't contain live microorganisms that are essential and beneficial to our health. All real food – fruits, vegetables, meat, dairy, etc. – contains some live bacteria (until they are processed). Why can't we just live on specially formulated shakes that have 'all the vitamins and minerals that we need' and thrive? Because it's still dead food. Everything you eat (other than on the odd special occasion) should be 'useful' to your body, so next time you pick up a piece of food, ask yourself, 'Is this providing me/my body with useful nutrients?'

LEAFY GREENS.
If there is one food we could all do with eating more of it is leafy greens. They contain an abundance of health-protective compounds, antioxidants, vitamins and minerals – everything from vitamin A, C and K to loads of potassium and folate. Make sure you have some leafy greens, whether in a salad or a smoothie, every day. Another benefit of getting used to eating greens every day is that it can help reduce cravings for sweet foods – because leafy greens contain slightly bitter compounds they naturally reduce your sweetness tolerance. So go for gold with adding more greens to your day!

M

MINDSET.
Don't 'diet'. People who diet consistently tend to gain more weight over time, and it doesn't do any good for your body or your mind. Instead of going on a diet, make it your goal to gain more energy, feel better, healthier, happier and fitter. Focus on nourishing your body instead of depriving it and weight loss will end up being a natural side effect. In other words, think about what foods you need to add for health instead of subtract.

Diets make us feel deprived and guilty for having things we 'shouldn't' and this negative mentality doesn't do us any good, nor is it sustainable. Take the 'glass is half full' approach instead and focus on all the things you should be eating for great health and nourishment and it will leave little room for less healthy things, and make way for a much more positive, happier mind and body!

MINDFUL EATING.
Mindless eating is where the calories can easily stack up without you even realising. Picking at a few chips, nuts or biscuits here and there throughout the day can easily add up to a full meal. It's good practice to always put a portion on a plate (even if it's just a cracker or one cookie), then put leftovers or the rest away. This way your mind will consciously register what (and how much) you're eating. Mindful eating means consciously stopping for a few seconds to think if you really need this snack or second helping, or if it's going to provide you with useful nutrients (or actually give you some pleasure or not), before you put it into your mouth on auto-pilot.

N

NUMBER TWOS.
The importance of having a well-functioning gut that eliminates waste and toxins in a timely manner cannot be underestimated. If you're not doing your 'number twos' regularly you feel, excuse the pun, crap – lethargic, irritable, unsettled and sluggish. It even has an impact on your hunger levels and what you eat.

Constipation (when you're going less than every 2 days or less than three times per week) is a pretty common problem for many. However, it is not normal. Many people have come to rely on different types of laxatives, coffee being one of the most popular! Sometimes it could be due to a hormonal shift, such as in pregnancy, or with an underactive thyroid, and some medications interfere with bowel motility. To help get things moving along regularly:
– Eat a high-fibre diet (see 'F' for Fibre).
– Drink plenty of fluids. You need adequate fluid for the fibre in your system to actually work and flush things out (see 'H' for Hydrate).
– Move every hour you're awake, especially if you're at a desk job. Movement stimulates bowel peristalsis (a wave-like movement); being sedentary inhibits it. That's why most people are often bunged up after a long-haul flight and it takes them a while to get back to their normal bowel habits/routine.

– Relax. It's a bit of a 'chicken and egg' scenario, where anxiety can cause poor bowel movements (because during periods of anxiety your body prioritises other functions), but conversely poor bowel routine also causes anxiety. So if you do think that consistent/persistent low-level stress could be contributing to unsatisfactory bowel habits, prioritise working on stress levels.

– Eat less highly processed foods. The problem with highly processed foods, other than the fact that they are generally devoid of important nutrients (that have been stripped during factory processing), is that they are 'dead' foods. They're not live foods, i.e., they don't contain live microorganisms that are essential and beneficial to our health, including our gut health (see 'L' for Love Real Food).

– If needed, a mixture of psyllium husk and flaxseed (or LSA) can help with keeping you regular. Mix equal quantities of psyllium husk and LSA or flaxseed and keep in a zip-lock bag in the fridge and add 2–3 teaspoons to your breakfast muesli/No-grainola or a smoothie or water. Alpine tea also works!

NUTRITIOUS CARBS.

While reducing the amount of carbohydrates you eat can help you lose weight, you still need some – if you cut carbs out completely you'd be missing out on a whole lot of nutritious foods, like fruit, and lots of different vegetables, legumes and grains, and therefore many of the great vitamins, minerals and fibre they provide. The key is portion control and being smart with what types of carbohydrates you choose. Remember, the least processed carbs are more nutritious – opt for more starchy vegetables (such as kumara, carrots, pumpkin, peas, parsnips, potato, etc.) as your carbohydrate base, followed by legumes and wholegrains (such as beans, lentils, bulghur, brown rice, etc.), and lastly having some of the more processed carbs (such as pasta, white rice, couscous, etc.) every now and again is fine.

O

BE A LITTLE ORGANISED.

A little organisation goes a long way to make healthy eating throughout the week easier, and the easier things are to do, the more likely you are to do them! Plan your meals for the week (or even better, get the Fresh Start bag if you can) and freeze some meals that you can draw upon for busy nights. Pre-chop and freeze smoothie ingredients such as banana, cauliflower, avocado, etc. and keep in zip-lock bags for instant, nutritious smoothies. Soup can be made in advance and frozen in portions for a great low-calorie, satisfying lunch or dinner. Many of the snacks in this book are suitable for freezing too.

P

PROTEIN.

Protein is the ultimate fill-you-up food, helping to satisfy hunger and keep you fuller for longer. It's more satiating than carbohydrates and fats, and it also helps to preserve and build muscle mass (and a higher muscle mass means a faster metabolism!). So make sure to include some good quality, lean protein at most meals. Check out page 15 to get to know your protein foods.

Q

QUALITY OVER QUANTITY.

It's important that you still enjoy your favourite foods. We'd never ask you to cut out your favourite ice cream or chocolate entirely because that just wouldn't be any fun! Instead, be smart about how you choose and eat your favourite foods. Go for quality over quantity – buy a small (25–50g) bar of good-quality chocolate instead of a large block. By savouring a small amount, you can still enjoy your favourite foods: the key is moderation.

QUIT (OR CUT DOWN ON) CAFFEINE AND ALCOHOL.

Don't freak out and think you'll never be allowed a cup of coffee or glass of wine ever again; however, if you are a coffee or alcohol drinker, chances are you could do with reducing the amount you have (most people would benefit from significantly reducing their intake). While cutting down on caffeine can be a tad painful at first, with withdrawal symptoms such as headaches, the benefits will likely soon become apparent with you feeling calmer and having more real (not nervous) energy. You'll also improve the quality of your sleep (caffeine has a half-life of 8 hours, so if you are drinking it after 11am-ish it'll be affecting your sleep – often without you knowing it). Reducing your intake will also reduce your adrenal output (of the 'fight or flight' hormones adrenaline and cortisol), putting less pressure on your adrenal glands, which get worked so hard in today's fast-paced life as it is! If you are a coffee drinker, aim to have no more than 1 cup a day.

There is now so much evidence supporting the link between alcohol and many cancers that a regular intake is just not worth it. On top of that, it's well known that heavy drinking weakens the immune system due to the body having to divert resources (and nutrients) to processing and metabolising the alcohol rather than towards other functions of your immunity.

Save alcohol only for special occasions, and a maximum of 2–3 standard drinks at that. It'll take a lot of pressure off your liver which, like your adrenal glands, is overworked already these days with the amount of toxins (such as pollution, skin products, chemicals, processed foods, etc.) it already has to process. If it's become a regular thing throughout the week – some people believe a glass of wine in the evening relaxes them – consider switching to something else that 'relaxes' you (a cup of tea, a gentle walk, etc.). Alcohol is a stimulant (not a relaxant), so even if you feel it helps you 'nod off' easier, it does impact the quality of your sleep by interfering with REM sleep (the very deep stage of sleep). That's why even if you've only had one or two drinks the night before, you don't feel as vibrant/alert the next morning even if you've had a decent length of sleep.

R

REST AND RELAX.

Sleep deprivation induces over-production of the appetite-stimulating hormone ghrelin (and under-produces the satiating hormone leptin, which tells you you're full). So getting enough sleep and feeling well rested are essential for being able to lose weight efficiently and keep it off. Good-quality sleep is a strong factor linked to successful weight loss and maintenance. So set yourself up for success by getting at least 8 hours of sleep a night, ideally with at least two hours before midnight.

For good sleep, don't drink alcohol during the week and limit caffeine to 1 cup before 11am-ish. Have a cool room (around 18°C) and no screens at least 30 minutes before bed time. Turn off electronic devices or set to flight mode so you don't get woken up or are exposed to any bright/artificial lights (e.g. from your clock). If you get into a good routine with your sleep habits, your body will find a natural rhythm of producing melatonin at the right time to make you relaxed and sleepy, and serotonin at the right time to naturally wake you up. Even if you aren't able to get to sleep by the right time (on the odd occasion), still try to wake up around your normal wake-up time to keep in sync.

Being calm and relaxed is important for our health in more ways than you might realise. Prolonged stress (caused by the business and pressures of work, social and family life) can result in adrenaline and cortisol production. The best thing you can do every day to keep your body in a relaxed state (even if things do get a little crazy) is to breathe deeply through your diaphragm (and not in short breaths through your chest). Take 5 minutes out of your day (perhaps after work, first thing in the morning, or in the evening) to just lie on your back and concentrate on your breathing. Take regular breaks from technology (e.g. screens, social media, phones etc.) too – at the very least a few hours at a time a few times a week – you'll find a new sense of freedom and relaxation.

A relaxed attitude to food is key to having a healthy relationship with it, which means having treats every now and again – whether it's a glass of wine with friends, popcorn at the movies or an ice cream at the beach. It's good to have things that give you pleasure and not feel 'guilty' about it – be happy that you can live a little and relax about something so small in the grand scheme of things! It's what you do most of the time that counts, not what you do on the odd occasion.

S

SNACKING.

If you find three good meals a day isn't quite enough, add in a couple of nutritious snacks throughout the day to get you from one meal to the next. Snacks are a great opportunity to get even more goodness into your diet – base at least one of your snacks around fresh vegetables and/or fruit and any others on other nutrient-dense foods like nuts, seeds, yoghurt, etc. There's lots of great snack recipes and ideas on pages 199–200 (chapter 5). Make some in bulk and freeze them so that you can take them to work or have them ready for when you get home.

SUPPLEMENTS.

Are supplements necessary? If you're eating a highly nutritious, well-varied diet, then possibly not. However, taking some can't hurt; view them as nutritional insurance, a little 'top-up'. While they'll never be able to replace a nutritious diet, they can help supplement an already good diet to double check you're covering all your bases. It's a good idea to get your iron and zinc levels tested (considering sub-optimal levels are relatively common), a B-vitamin supplement every now and again can be helpful, too. For vitamin D (another very important vitamin that a significant number of people are low in), get enough safe sun exposure every day.

T

TRAIN AND TUNE YOUR TASTE BUDS.

Reducing the amount of sugars and refined (highly processed) carbohydrates you eat will help train your body to avoid using these as your primary source of fuel and instead start feeding off your fat stores. Your taste buds will also eventually tune and adapt, and you'll find you have less of a craving for sweet foods.

Eating some leafy greens every day can help reduce sweet cravings too; because they contain slightly bitter compounds, they naturally reduce your tolerance for sweetness.

U

UNREFINED VS REFINED SUGARS.

If you're wondering about refined sugars vs unrefined/ natural sweeteners, here's what you need to know. Both should be cut down on/only eaten in very small quantities as they're equally calorific and raise blood sugar levels. However, the difference with unrefined sweeteners such as honey or pure maple syrup is that you do get some vitamins and minerals (but still not enough to justify eating much!) instead of just empty calories. All recipes in the Fresh Start bag are refined-sugar-free and in this book we have also given you the option of using refined-sugar-free ingredients and sauces. Fresh and dried fruit such as dates, bananas, dried apricots etc. are a great way to sweeten things up without the use of refined sugars. We like to use these naturally sweet and nutritious ingredients in lots of our treats and baking.

V

VEGGIES.

There is one food that you can eat as much of as you like, and that's non-starchy (non-carby) vegetables! In general, these are the most vibrant, colourful vegetables that have a high water and fibre content – think anything from cucumber to tomato, capsicum, cabbage, cauliflower, broccoli, etc.; the list is long. These types of vegetables are super-packed full of amazing vitamins and minerals, yet are very low in calories – so it's a total win–win situation! Aim to have some at every meal (and snack) – that means adding in some vegetables at breakfast. Sautéed spinach and tomatoes with your eggs, vegetables in your smoothie and as snacks with a dip are just some ways of upping your veg intake throughout the day. Let them become the main part of your snacks and meals. The more the better!

W

WEIGHING YOURSELF.

Avoid weighing yourself too often – no more than once per week (even once every 2–3 weeks is sufficient) – as your weight will fluctuate daily and you don't want an arbitrary number on the scales to get you down and sabotage your efforts. Fluctuations in body weight naturally occur as your body adjusts, and if you're gaining muscle but losing fat it is possible your weight may not change much to begin with (as muscle weighs more than fat). So it's much better to go by how you feel and how your clothes fit. Weigh yourself at the same time every day (e.g. first thing in the morning, on the same day of the week and in the same clothes/or without).

WRITE IT DOWN.

The act of simply writing down what you eat and drink can be immensely helpful to make you more aware of what, how much and when you're eating. It's a great practice to do for a week or two to get a good gauge on your eating habits, and help you highlight the pain points of your day of eating, so you can focus on making the best choices, and being prepared around these times of the day (or week).

Y

YUM.

Make nutritious food yum! Adding loads of punchy flavour to your food, from spices to zesty marinades, will stimulate your taste buds and be more satisfying than bland food, and you won't feel the need to eat as much.

Z

ZINC.

Zinc plays a key role in fighting infection, your immune response and also wound healing, fertility (with your sex hormones), growth and neurological function. Signs of zinc deficiency include having a susceptibility to colds and flus, white flecks in your nails and hair loss, but you don't always see these signs if it's more mild.

It's a good idea to get your iron and zinc levels tested (considering sub-optimal levels are relatively common and not routinely tested for). It used to be easier to meet our zinc requirements because it was more available in our soil. However, with the rise of conventional farming practices most soil used for food production in New Zealand is now deficient in zinc, unless it has actively been added back. And if it's not in the soil, it's not going to be in our food. The best sources of zinc are good-quality beef, lamb, liver and, from plant sources, seeds, particularly sunflower and pumpkin seeds, and to a lesser extent in eggs and legumes, but it's not a bad idea to consider taking a supplement.

chapter one—

breakfast

- *Get a head start with your 5+ a day.* Add some vegetables to your breakfast. Try spinach or tomatoes with your eggs or some greens or cauliflower in a smoothie – just some ways to get more veg into your day!

- *Have some protein and make sure you eat enough.* Remember, protein keeps you feeling fuller for longer and it has a low glycaemic index. So make sure you include some protein (and also fat, which does the same) at brekkie, whether it's from eggs, yoghurt, cheese, milk, avocado, nuts, salmon, beans, etc. Eggs deserve a special shout-out as the perfect breakfast food!

- *Rehydrate.* You've gone a whole night without liquids, so make sure you hydrate well in the morning to avoid dehydration – have a smoothie and/or a couple of glasses of water or herbal tea. You'll feel much more alert if you're well hydrated. A cup of warm water with a little apple cider vinegar (ACV) or lemon juice is a great way to help get your digestive system working.

- *Mix it up.* Many of us like routine with breakfast and don't mind having the same thing every day, but try to change it up at least once or twice throughout the week. If you're an eggs person, try having something else on a couple of days, or if you don't usually have eggs, give them a go. Remember, variety is key!

- *Don't leave it too late.* Try to eat within about 1 hour of waking. However, if you struggle to eat first thing in the morning, take your brekkie to work, or just have something small like a piece of fruit or a smoothie and eat within 1–2 hours after that.

40. APPLE AND APRICOT PUFF MUESLI.

Makes:	10 portions (¾ cup per portion)
Prep time:	10 minutes
Cook time:	15 minutes

3 tablespoons coconut oil
2 tablespoons maple syrup
2 tablespoons honey
1½ teaspoons mixed spice
¾ teaspoon ground cinnamon
1½ cups brown rice puffs
1½ cups millet puffs
1 cup quinoa puffs or flakes
½ cup sunflower seeds
½ cup pumpkin seeds
½ cup coconut flakes/chips
¾ cup flaked almonds
½–¾ cup chopped dried apple
⅓ cup chopped dried apricots

To serve
Natural unsweetened yoghurt
    or coconut yoghurt
Milk of your choice (e.g. cows,
    almond, rice, soy)
Seasonal fruit

This light, gluten-free muesli has the warm spices and fruitiness of an apple or apricot crumble. Feel free to mix and match the total 4 cups of puffs as you like or even use only one type of puff. Some rolled oats can also be used in place of the puffs for a non-gluten-free version.

Preheat oven to 180°C. Line an oven tray with baking paper.

1. In a small pot, combine coconut oil, maple syrup, honey, mixed spice and cinnamon. Place on low heat and stir until everything is melted and combined.

2. In a large bowl, combine brown rice puffs, millet puffs, quinoa puffs, sunflower seeds, pumpkin seeds, coconut and flaked almonds. Pour in the coconut oil mixture and toss well to combine.

3. Pour half the mixture onto the lined tray and spread out in a single layer. Bake, tossing once during cooking, for about 8 minutes or until puffs are lightly golden. Remove from oven, transfer to a large bowl and repeat with the second batch of muesli.

4. Allow muesli to cool completely, then stir through dried fruit.

Serve with yoghurt, milk and seasonal fruit. The muesli will keep for a few weeks in an airtight container in the fridge.

GF   V   DF (serve w/coconut yoghurt and DF milk)

Energy	289kcal (1206kJ)
Protein	7.2g
Carbohydrate	23.4g (10.8g sugars)
Fat	18.4g (7.5g sat fat)

AVOCADO ON TOAST.

Avocado on toast is one of life's most simple and delicious pleasures, and it's a bonus that avocado is so good for you too! Here are some easy ways to have this superfood fave as a quick brekkie or lunch. Serve on thin wholegrain toast, or the Seed Loaf on page 252.

MEXICAN AVO ON TOAST WITH CORN AND CAPSICUM.

Makes:	**1 portion**
Prep time:	**10 minutes**

¼ small (or ⅛ medium) red onion, thinly sliced
1 tablespoon red wine or apple cider vinegar
Flesh of ¼ firm ripe avocado
¼ teaspoon Mexican Seasoning (store-bought or see page 256)
2 thin slices toasted grainy bread (or Seed Loaf on page 252)
½ roasted capsicum, sliced (from a jar or the deli)
1–2 tablespoons corn kernels (fresh, raw, canned or defrosted frozen)
½ teaspoon black sesame seeds or pepitas (optional)

You could also use store-bought sauerkraut in place of the pickled onion.

1. In a small bowl, toss red onion with vinegar. Set aside to marinate for at least 5 minutes before draining.
2. Roughly mash together avocado, Mexican Seasoning and a pinch of flaky sea salt and spread over toast. Top with roasted capsicum, corn and pickled onions. Sprinkle with sesame seeds/pepitas (if using).

DF | V | GF (use seed loaf)

Energy	289kcal (1209kJ)
Protein	8g
Carbohydrate	32g (6.1g sugars)
Fat	13.3g (1.9g sat fat)

Makes:	1 portion
Prep time:	5 minutes

Good pinch each of curry
    powder, caraway or cumin
    seeds and flaky sea salt
Flesh of ¼ firm ripe avocado, sliced
2 thin slices toasted grainy bread
    (or Seed Loaf on page 252)
1 soft or hard-boiled free-
    range egg, sliced
Small handful of watercress,
    microgreens or rocket

1. Combine curry powder, caraway or cumin seeds and salt in a small bowl. Top toast with avocado slices and boiled egg. Sprinkle with curried salt seasoning and garnish with greens.

DF | V | GF (use seed loaf)

Energy	301kcal (1258kJ)
Protein	13.1g
Carbohydrate	24.2g (2.5g sugars)
Fat	15.8g (2.8g sat fat)

48.

AVO ON TOAST WITH PAPRIKA MUSHROOMS AND PINE NUTS.

Makes:	1 portion
Prep time:	5 minutes
Cook time:	5 minutes

1 teaspoon olive oil or butter
6–8 button mushrooms, sliced
1 teaspoon pine nuts
Good pinch of smoked paprika
Good pinch of cumin seeds
2 thin slices toasted grainy bread
    (or Seed Loaf on page 252)
Flesh of ¼ firm ripe avocado
Chopped coriander or parsley,
    to garnish

1. Heat olive oil or butter in a small fry-pan on medium heat. Cook mushrooms, pine nuts, smoked paprika and cumin, with a good pinch of flaky sea salt, for about 2 minutes or until just coloured – add a teaspoon or two of water to the pan to help soften the mushrooms if needed.

2. Mash avocado with a little salt and pepper and spread over toast. Top with the smoky mushrooms and pine nuts. Garnish with coriander or parsley.

V	DF (use oil)	GF (use seed loaf)		

Energy	317kcal (1323kJ)
Protein	9.9g
Carbohydrate	24.5g (2.8g sugars)
Fat	18.3g (2.8g sat fat)

AVO ON TOAST WITH SMOKED FISH, TOMATO AND BASIL.

Makes:	1 portion
Prep time:	5 minutes

Flesh of ¼ firm ripe avocado
2 thin slices toasted grainy bread
    (or Seed Loaf on page 252)
100g smoked fish, salmon or
    canned tuna (drained), flaked
6 cherry tomatoes, cut in half
1 teaspoon sweet chilli sauce
    (store-bought or see page 258)
2–3 basil leaves, sliced, or baby
    basil leaves
1 wedge lemon

1. Mash avocado with a little salt and pepper and spread over toast. Top with smoked fish/salmon/tuna.

2. Toss tomatoes with sweet chilli sauce and basil and spoon over. Season with flaky sea salt and cracked black pepper and squeeze over lemon just before eating.

DF	GF (use seed loaf)

Energy	364kcal (1521kJ)
Protein	31.7g
Carbohydrate	27.3g (5.4g sugars)
Fat	13.2g (2.2g sat fat)

Makes:	1 portion
Prep time:	5 minutes
Cook time:	5 minutes

1 tablespoon balsamic vinegar
½ teaspoon honey
1 medium tomato
¼ teaspoon olive oil
1 rasher lean bacon (e.g. shoulder
   or middle eye), cut in half
2 thin slices toasted grainy bread
   (or Seed Loaf on page 252)
Flesh of ¼ firm ripe avocado, sliced
Chopped basil or coriander,
   to garnish

1. Combine balsamic vinegar and honey in a bowl. Cut tomato into 4 even slices and toss in the balsamic mixture. Set aside.

2. Heat olive oil in a small fry-pan and cook bacon for 2–3 minutes each side until crisp, remove from the pan, drain on paper towels and chop. Add marinated tomato slices to the pan and sear on each side until coloured. Top toast with avocado slices, balsamic tomatoes, a pinch of flaky sea salt and bacon. Garnish with basil or coriander.

DF | GF (use seed loaf)

Energy	340kcal (1423kJ)
Protein	10g
Carbohydrate	29.9g (8.2g sugars)
Fat	18.9g (4.2g sat fat)

CHORIZO BAKED BEANS
WITH SPINACH AND GRILLED CHEESE.

Makes:	4 portions
Prep time:	10 minutes
Cook time:	20 minutes

100g chorizo, sliced or diced
1 onion, diced
1 red, orange or yellow
    capsicum, cored and diced,
    or 1 medium courgette, diced
1 teaspoon smoked paprika
1 tablespoon thyme leaves
1 x 400g can cannellini beans,
    rinsed and drained
1 x 400g can kidney beans,
    rinsed and drained
1 x 400g can crushed tomatoes
    (preferably with garlic and
    chilli)
2 tablespoons Worcestershire
    sauce
1 tablespoon chipotle sauce
1 tablespoon tomato relish
    or chutney
2 handfuls chopped spinach,
    silverbeet or baby spinach
75g crumbled feta or
    goat's cheese or ¼ cup
    grated cheese
Basil leaves, to garnish

Canned baked beans have a reputation for being high in salt and sugar, so here's our scrumptious, freshened-up version packed with delicious smoky and savoury flavours, fresh herbs and vegetables. It's one of those meals you could happily eat for breakfast, lunch or dinner.

Preheat oven to grill.

1. Place chorizo in a medium fry-pan (use an ovenproof one if you've got one) on medium heat – the chorizo will start heating up and sizzling. Cook for 1–2 minutes, then add onion and capsicum/courgette and continue cooking for a few minutes until onion is soft.

2. Add paprika, thyme, beans, tomatoes, Worcestershire sauce, chipotle sauce, tomato relish/chutney and spinach/silverbeet. Stir and simmer for 5–8 minutes until thickened. Season to taste with salt and pepper.

3. If using an ovenproof fry-pan, sprinkle cheese over and place under grill for a few minutes until bubbly. Alternatively, transfer beans to an ovenproof dish and sprinkle cheese over the top before grilling.

Serve hot, garnished with basil, with a poached egg on top if you like.

GF (use GF Worcestershire sauce) | DF (omit cheese)

Energy	293kcal (1224kJ)
Protein	19.7g
Carbohydrate	33.5g (10g sugars)
Fat	6.4g (2.4g sat fat)

PB 'N' J BREAKFAST JARS
WITH BANANA, RASPBERRY CHIA JAM
AND NUT BUTTER YOGHURT.

53.

Makes:	4 portions
Prep time:	10 minutes

Chia jam

1½ cups frozen raspberries or
strawberries, defrosted
1½ tablespoons chia seeds

Nut butter yoghurt

2 cups natural, unsweetened
yoghurt or coconut yoghurt
3 tablespoons smooth nut
butter (e.g. almond, cashew
or peanut)
1½ tablespoons maple syrup
1 teaspoon vanilla bean paste
or extract

To assemble

¼ cup chopped nuts
(e.g. hazelnuts, almonds,
pecans, etc.)
2 tablespoons coconut chips
or threads
1 tablespoon cacao nibs
(optional)
1 ripe banana, peeled
and sliced

If you're a peanut butter and jelly fan, you'll love the flavours in this simple brekkie – sweet and tart raspberry chia jam, sliced banana and nut butter-flavoured yoghurt. You'll also be doing your insides a big favour with all the fibre, prebiotic and probiotic goodness contained within!

1. To make chia jam, in a bowl, mash together defrosted berries and chia seeds. Set aside.

2. To make nut butter yoghurt, whisk yoghurt, nut butter, maple syrup and vanilla together in a bowl.

3. In a medium dry fry-pan, toast nuts and coconut together on medium heat for about 2 minutes until golden. Transfer to a small bowl and mix in cacao nibs (if using).

4. In serving glasses or jars, layer chia jam, nut butter yoghurt and banana, and sprinkle with toasted nut mixture.

GF | V | DF (use coconut yoghurt)

Energy	257kcal (1076kJ)
Protein	11.9g
Carbohydrate	22.3g (14.9g sugars)
Fat	12.4g (3.2g sat fat)

Makes:	10 portions
	(½ cup per portion)
Prep time:	5 minutes
Cook time:	12–15 minutes

1 cup shredded or thread
   coconut
½ cup raw almonds
½ cup macadamias
8–10 pitted medjool dates,
   chopped
½ cup sunflower seeds
½ cup pumpkin seeds
Zest of 1 lemon
Zest of 1 orange
1½ teaspoons mixed spice
¾ teaspoon ground cinnamon
¼ teaspoon ground ginger or
   ground cardamom (optional)
½ teaspoon salt
3 tablespoons melted
   coconut oil
1 tablespoon honey or
   maple syrup

To serve
Natural unsweetened yoghurt
   or coconut yoghurt
Milk of your choice (e.g. cows,
   almond, rice, soy)
Seasonal fruit

This grain- and gluten-free granola is packed with nuts and seeds and flavoured with warming spices, lemon and orange zest so it's full of delicious goodness. Feel free to add some freeze-dried fruit (such as raspberries, feijoas or plums) to the no-grainola, once it has completely cooled, to vary the flavour.

Preheat oven to 180°C. Line a large oven tray with baking paper.

1. Place coconut, almonds, macadamias and dates in a food processor and blitz until combined and crumbly, much like crumble topping.

2. Transfer to a bowl and stir in remaining ingredients.

3. Spread mixture out on the lined tray in a single layer. Bake, tossing once during cooking, for 12–15 minutes until the no-grainola is light golden. Allow no-grainola to cool completely.

Serve with yoghurt, milk and seasonal fruit. The no-grainola will keep for up to 6 weeks in an airtight container in the fridge.

GF | V | DF (serve w/coconut yoghurt and DF milk)

Energy	404kcal (1689kJ)
Protein	8.6g
Carbohydrate	20.8g (17.6g sugars)
Fat	30.9g (11.2g sat fat)

Makes:	2 portions
Prep time:	10 minutes
Cook time:	15 minutes

Roast mushrooms and tomatoes

2 teaspoons balsamic vinegar
1 teaspoon honey
2 teaspoons olive oil
1 teaspoon chopped thyme
1 clove garlic, finely chopped
4 large (or 6 medium)
　　Portobello mushrooms, stalks
　　trimmed or removed
½ punnet cherry tomatoes

To serve

1 teaspoon butter or olive oil
3 large handfuls chopped
　　spinach or baby spinach
4 free-range eggs
2 tablespoons Herb and
　　Cashew Pesto (store-bought
　　or see page 258), slightly
　　warmed or at room temp

This makes a delicious brunch, and a great, healthy way to start off your weekend!

Preheat oven to 200°C. Bring a full kettle of water to the boil.

1. In a small bowl, mix balsamic vinegar, honey, olive oil, thyme and garlic together. Arrange mushrooms, gill-side up, in a medium-large baking dish. Drizzle over balsamic mixture, and season with salt and pepper. Scatter tomatoes around mushrooms. Roast for 12–15 minutes until mushrooms are soft and tomatoes are starting to blister.

2. Heat butter/olive oil in a fry-pan on medium heat. Add spinach and cook, stirring, for 1–2 minutes until bright green and wilted. Season with a little salt and pepper.

3. Pour boiling water into a separate fry-pan or pot and bring to a simmer on medium heat. Carefully crack in eggs and poach for about 1–2 minutes until whites are just set but yolks are still runny, or a little longer until done to your liking.

To serve, place 2–3 roast mushrooms and half of the tomatoes on each plate, top with spinach, poached eggs seasoned with salt and pepper, and spoon pesto on top.

GF | V | DF (use DF pesto)

Energy	313kcal (1310kJ)
Protein	18.3g
Carbohydrate	6.7g (5.9g sugars)
Fat	22.9g (4.8g sat fat)

BROCCOLI, CAPSICUM AND FETA OMELETTE.

Makes:	2 portions
Prep time:	5 minutes
Cook time:	10 minutes

1 teaspoon olive oil
1 small or ½ medium red onion, finely diced
4–5 large florets broccoli, thinly sliced
4 free-range eggs
¼ cup milk
½ roasted capsicum, sliced (from a jar or the deli)
50g feta or goat's cheese, crumbled
2 tablespoons roughly chopped flat-leaf parsley
1 small red chilli, seeds removed and thinly sliced (optional)

Packed full of protein, vitamins and minerals, eggs are always a great breakfast choice, and even more so when you can add in some vegetables, bumping up your veggie intake for the day before it's even started!

Bring a half kettle of water to the boil.

1. Heat oil in a small-to-medium non-stick fry-pan on medium heat and cook onion for 2–3 minutes on gentle heat until softened.

2. Place broccoli in a heatproof bowl and cover with boiling water. Leave for 1–2 minutes until bright green and just-tender, then drain well.

3. Meanwhile, whisk eggs and milk together in a bowl or jug and season with salt and pepper.

4. Pour egg mixture over onions, stir once, then allow to settle without stirring for 1–2 minutes and top with the broccoli, roasted capsicum and half the feta/goat's cheese. Gently lift the egg up on one side from underneath and fold in half, enclosing the filling. Allow to cook a further 2–3 minutes.

Cut in half and transfer to serving plates. Sprinkle with remaining cheese, parsley and chilli (if using) before serving.

GF | V

Energy	269kcal (1125kJ)
Protein	21.8g
Carbohydrate	7.7g (6.1g sugars)
Fat	16.3g (6.3g sat fat)

Makes:	1 portion (double, triple or quadruple quantities to suit)
Prep time:	5 minutes
Cook time:	2 minutes

8 spears asparagus
1 free-range egg
Squeeze of lemon juice
½ teaspoon extra-virgin olive oil
50g cold smoked salmon

Just three ingredients, that go so perfectly together.

Bring a full kettle of water to the boil and bring a small pot of water to a simmer.

1. Snap or cut tough ends off asparagus and place spears in a heatproof bowl or pot. Pour over boiling water to cover and leave to sit for about 2 minutes until bright green and just tender.

2. Meanwhile, carefully crack egg into simmering water. Poach for 1–2 minutes or until white is just set and yolk is still runny.

3. Drain asparagus, place on serving plate and drizzle with lemon juice, extra-virgin olive oil and a pinch of sea salt.

To serve, scoop poached egg out of water with a slotted spoon, drain on paper towels and place on top of asparagus. Arrange slices of smoked salmon beside. Season egg with salt and pepper.

Energy	222kcal (929kJ)
Protein	20.5g
Carbohydrate	3.6g (3.5g sugars)
Fat	13.6g (2.3g sat fat)

FLUFFY RICOTTA PANCAKES WITH FEIJOA, CITRUS AND HONEY.

Makes:	4 portions (12 pancakes)
Prep time:	10 minutes
Cook time:	25 minutes

½ cup milk
2 free-range eggs, separated
3 tablespoons runny honey
Finely grated zest of 1 lemon
    or orange
½ cup GF or wholemeal flour
1 teaspoon baking powder
200g soft creamy ricotta
    cheese
3 teaspoons coconut oil,
    for cooking

To serve
4 tablespoons unsweetened
    natural yoghurt or coconut
    yoghurt
4 ripe feijoas, flesh scooped
    out and sliced
1–2 teaspoons runny honey

I'm willing to bet these are THE fluffiest pancakes you will ever eat. It's all thanks to whipping the egg whites and folding them through the batter, keeping them super light. They're also high in protein, and much lower in carbs than other pancakes. If feijoas aren't in season, serve with a ripe peach, a couple of apricots, or even a banana.

1. In a large mixing bowl, whisk milk, egg yolks (reserve whites in a separate clean bowl), honey, citrus zest, flour, baking powder and a good pinch of salt together until well combined. Lightly whisk in ricotta – leaving it a little lumpy is fine.

2. Whisk egg whites until soft peaks form. Fold into ricotta mixture using a large metal spoon, keeping mixture nice and light.

3. Heat 1 teaspoon coconut oil in a large non-stick fry-pan on low-medium heat. Cook pancakes (about 2 tablespoons of mixture per pancake) for a few minutes on one side, before flipping delicately with a spatula to cook for a further 2–3 minutes on other side or until puffed and golden. You should be able to cook 4 pancakes at a time so you'll be doing three batches and adding coconut oil in between batches. Transfer to a plate and keep warm.

To serve, divide pancakes between plates, top with a dollop of yoghurt, sliced feijoa and drizzle over a little honey.

Energy	279kcal (1166kJ)
Protein	12g
Carbohydrate	30.5g (20.6g sugars)
Fat	11.8g (7.3g sat fat)

ROSEMARY, HAM AND
PARMESAN SCRAMBLE.

Makes:	2 portions
Prep time:	2 minutes
Cook time:	3 minutes

1 teaspoon olive oil
4 free-range eggs
½ cup milk
½ teaspoon finely chopped
   rosemary leaves
100g shaved or diced ham
¼ cup grated Parmesan cheese
1 large handful baby spinach
   leaves or ¾ cup finely sliced
   kale (tough stalks removed)

Treat yourself to some extra-delicious scrambled eggs.

1. Heat oil in a medium non-stick fry-pan on medium heat. While pan heats up, whisk eggs and milk with a fork in a jug or bowl and season with salt and pepper.
2. Pour egg mixture into heated pan and gently stir with a wooden spoon for 1–2 minutes, bringing the outside egg into the centre so it cooks evenly. When the eggs start to clump together, sprinkle with rosemary, ham, Parmesan and spinach/kale and gently fold the mixture together. Spoon straight onto plates and serve.

GF

Energy   266kcal (1113kJ)
Protein   28.3g
Carbohydrate   4.1g (3.9g sugars)
Fat   15.3g (5.2g sat fat)

PEAR, CHIA AND RASPBERRY BIRCHER.

Makes:	1 portion (but can be easily doubled)
Prep time:	5 minutes + at least 1 hour chilling time

Bircher

⅓ cup rolled oats
2½ teaspoons chia seeds
½ cup milk (e.g. cows, soy, rice, almond)
½ teaspoon vanilla bean paste or extract
2 teaspoons maple syrup or honey
½ teaspoon ground cinnamon
1 ripe pear, grated

To serve

⅓ cup raspberries (fresh or defrosted)
1 tablespoon chopped pistachios or lightly toasted flaked almonds

Here's a quick, delicious breakfast you can make the night before. Feel free to mix it up with either pear or apple (or even mashed banana), which helps to naturally sweeten it. It's simply delish.

1. In a bowl, stir all bircher ingredients together. Cover with a plate and leave in the fridge for at least 1 hour or overnight.

2. When ready to eat, spoon into a bowl (if it is very thick, you may need to stir in a little milk to loosen it) and top with raspberries and pistachios/almonds.

V	DF (use DF milk)

Energy	379kcal (1586kJ)
Protein	12.2g
Carbohydrate	55.7g (32.3g sugars)
Fat	10.1g (10.1g sat fat)

chapter two—

soups, salads & lunch boxes

- *Avoid the 'post-lunch slump'* by avoiding highly processed/refined carbs (which have a high glycaemic index) and/or too many carbs at lunch time. This will help to prevent the blood glucose (and subsequent insulin) spike that is followed by a drop in blood glucose (the 'slump') and feelings of tiredness.

- Instead, *fill up on high-fibre foods (i.e. lots of vegetables), some protein and fat,* which take much longer for the body to break down, process and absorb, therefore giving you a much more sustained energy release, and just a small portion of minimally processed, low GI and fibre-rich carbs.

- *Soup* makes a tasty, convenient and healthy lunch. Make a big batch and freeze in individual portions (in zip-lock bags or containers) to take to work. It will be defrosted by lunch time and then all you have to do is heat it up.

- *Love your leftovers* and turn them into delicious, nutritious lunch boxes! It's a great idea to cook extra roast vegetables, quinoa, brown/wild rice, bulghur, noodles, etc. at dinner time that you can store in a container in the fridge to use in your salads over a few days. There's plenty of recipes in this section that are leftover friendly.

- *Buddy up with a work mate* who wants a healthy lunch (and less effort) every day, too, and take turns making and bringing lunches for both of you.

- If taking a salad to work or on the go, store dressing in a small jar or container (make sure the lid is secure to avoid spills!) and keep rest of salad separate in an airtight container. *Dress salad just before eating so it stays crisp and fresh.*

BROCCOLI AND PEANUT NOODLES WITH SESAME AVOCADO.

Makes:	**2 portions**
Prep time:	**10–15 minutes**
Cook time:	**5 minutes**

1 bunch (200–250g) broccolini
    or 1 medium head broccoli
1 bundle (80g) soba noodles
1½–2 cups shredded green
    cabbage or baby bok choy
¼–⅓ cup chopped roasted
    peanuts
1 tablespoon toasted
    sesame seeds
Flesh of 1 firm ripe avocado,
    halved

To serve
1 teaspoon extra-virgin olive oil
⅓ cup Asian Dressing
    (see page 256)
¼–½ cup chopped coriander
1 lime cut into wedges (optional)

The broccolini/broccoli in this dish is only lightly cooked so it still retains its freshness and a bit of crunch. Soba noodles overcook easily too, so be sure to time and taste test them while cooking and drain them as soon as they're done. To turn this into a more substantial, protein-packed meal, serve with a piece of seared salmon, chicken, some tofu or toss through a cup of edamame beans.

1. Bring a medium-to-large pot of water to the boil. If using broccolini, cut any with thicker stems in half lengthways; if using broccoli, chop into bite-sized florets. Boil broccolini/broccoli and noodles (snapped in half) for no more than 3 minutes (to avoid overcooking), drain, then run under cold water to stop the cooking process and drain again.

2. Toss broccolini/broccoli, noodles, cabbage/bok choy, peanuts and 1 teaspoon of the sesame seeds together. Sprinkle remaining toasted sesame seeds over avocado half.

3. When ready to serve, toss noodle salad with extra-virgin olive oil and dressing.

Divide salad and avocado between plates and scatter with coriander. Serve with lime wedges (if using) to squeeze over just before eating.

DF | V | GF (use GF soba noodles)

Energy	443kcal (1850kJ)
Protein	15.2g
Carbohydrate	38.3g (7.9g sugars)
Fat	23.2g (3.2g sat fat)

BUTTER CHICKEN SOUP
WITH ROASTED ROOT VEGETABLES,
COCONUT AND MINT AND LIME YOGHURT.

77.

Makes:	4 portions
Prep time:	25 minutes
Cook time:	30 minutes

Chicken

400–450g boneless, skinless
   chicken thighs
2 tablespoons Tandoori Paste
   (store-bought or see
   page 256)
1 teaspoon olive oil

Soup

300g peeled pumpkin, diced
200g orange kumara, peeled
   and diced
2 carrots, peeled and diced
1 teaspoon runny honey
4 teaspoons olive oil
1 leek
1 onion
1 tablespoon curry powder
1 tablespoon Tandoori Paste
   (store-bought or see
   page 256)
1 teaspoon smoked paprika
3 cups salt-reduced chicken
   stock
1 x 400g can crushed tomatoes
1 cup water
½ cup lite coconut milk

Mint and lime yoghurt

½ cup unsweetened natural
   yoghurt or coconut yoghurt
¼ cup chopped mint leaves
Juice of ½ lime or ¼ lemon

To serve

Coriander leaves (optional)

This dairy-free soup has got all the mild spicy flavours and creaminess butter chicken has, with natural sweetness from roasted pumpkin, kumara and carrots. Simply delicious with the mint and lime yoghurt!

Preheat oven to 220°C. Line an oven tray with baking paper.

1. Pat chicken dry with paper towels. Place in a bowl, coat in tandoori paste and set aside to marinate (at room temp) while you make the rest of the meal.

2. For the soup, toss pumpkin, kumara and carrots with honey and half the olive oil in prepared tray. Spread out in a single layer, season well with salt and pepper and roast for 20–25 minutes or until soft.

3. Meanwhile, finely dice leek and onion. Heat remaining olive oil in a large pot on medium heat. Cook leek and onion, with a good pinch of salt, for about 5 minutes or until soft (if sticking to the bottom of the pan and burning at any time, just stir in 1–2 tablespoons water, and it will unstick). Stir in curry powder, tandoori paste and smoked paprika and continue cooking for a further 1 minute.

4. Stir in stock, tomatoes, water and coconut milk; bring to a simmer. Add roasted vegetables and continue simmering for a few minutes. Use a stick blender, food processor or blender to purée until smooth, adding a bit more stock or water if you'd like a thinner soup. Season to taste with salt and pepper.

6. Heat olive oil for chicken in a large (preferably non-stick) fry-pan on medium-high heat. Season chicken with salt and cook for 6–8 minutes until just cooked through and golden on both sides. Set aside to rest for a few minutes before slicing or shredding meat with two forks.

7. Blend yoghurt, mint and lime/lemon juice until smooth and pale green. Season with salt. Alternatively, just finely chop mint and mix with yoghurt and lime/lemon juice. Thin out with a little water if needed.

To serve, ladle soup into bowls, top with shredded tandoori chicken and drizzle with mint and lime yoghurt. Garnish with coriander, if using.

Energy	387kcal (1619kJ)
Protein	28.8g
Carbohydrate	28.9g (19.8g sugars)
Fat	16g (5.9g sat fat)

SPICY CHIPOTLE CHICKEN AND QUINOA SOUP.

Makes:	6 portions
Prep time:	20 minutes
Cook time:	30 minutes

2 teaspoons olive oil
1 large onion, diced
1 clove garlic, finely chopped
2–3 stalks celery, finely diced
2 carrots, peeled and coarsely
    grated
1 tablespoon chopped thyme
2–3 tablespoons tomato paste
2–3 tablespoons chipotle sauce
1½ cups peeled and diced
    pumpkin or butternut
500g boneless, skinless
    chicken thighs
½ cup quinoa or brown rice
    or wild rice
1 litre salt-reduced chicken or
    vegetable stock
2½ cups water
½ teaspoon salt
Juice of 1 lime or ½ lemon

To serve
⅓ cup unsweetened natural
    yoghurt or lite sour cream
⅓ cup chopped coriander,
    basil or parsley

We're big fans of chipotle with its smoky, sweet and spicy Mexican flavour that instantly adds a flavour punch to any recipe, like this yummy chicken soup.

1. Heat olive oil in a large stock pot on medium heat. Cook onion, garlic, celery, carrot and thyme, with a good pinch of salt, for about 10 minutes until soft. If at any time the vegetables are beginning to stick to the bottom of the pot, just add a couple of tablespoons of water, stir, and they should unstick.

2. Stir in tomato paste and chipotle sauce, then add pumpkin/butternut, chicken thighs, quinoa/rice, stock, water and salt. Cover and bring to a simmer. Simmer for about 20 minutes or until grains are tender.

3. Using a slotted spoon, remove chicken pieces to a chopping board and finely dice or shred meat with two forks. Stir back into hot soup. Season to taste with lime or lemon juice, more salt, if needed, and freshly ground black pepper.

To serve, ladle into bowls, dollop with yoghurt/sour cream and scatter with fresh herbs.

GF | DF (omit yoghurt/sour cream)

Energy	209kcal (874kJ)
Protein	21.2g
Carbohydrate	15.1g (6g sugars)
Fat	6.5g (1.7g sat fat)

CHINESE CHICKEN AND CABBAGE SALAD
WITH GINGER, SOY, SESAME AND HONEY.

Makes:	2 portions
Prep time:	15–20 minutes
Cook time:	5 minutes

2 boneless, skinless chicken
    thighs (about 200g) or
    200–250g firm tofu
¾ teaspoon Chinese five-spice
    powder
1 teaspoon oil
2½–3 cups finely shredded
    cabbage (use either green
    cabbage or Chinese wong bok)
1 carrot, peeled and coarsely
    grated, shredded or julienned
3 spring onions, green part
    only, shredded
¼–½ cup chopped coriander
    (optional)
2 teaspoons toasted sesame seeds
1 teaspoon peeled and finely
    julienned fresh ginger
4–5 tablespoons Asian Dressing
    (see page 256)
2 tablespoons chopped roasted
    cashew nuts
½ lime, cut into wedges

Shredded cabbage, carrot and spring onion, tossed with delicious chicken coated in Chinese five-spice and a soy, sesame and honey dressing make a delicious, healthy lunch with lots of crunch and flavour. To speed things up even more you could use rotisserie chicken from the supermarket.

1. Pat chicken/tofu dry with paper towels and coat in five-spice powder. Season well with salt and pepper. Heat oil in a large fry-pan on medium-high heat. Cook chicken for about 5 minutes, or tofu for about 3 minutes, until cooked through and golden on all sides. Set chicken aside on a plate to rest for 5–10 minutes before slicing or shredding.

2. Toss chicken/tofu with all other salad ingredients (except dressing, cashew nuts and lime) and any resting juices from cooking the chicken. Just before eating, toss through dressing and sprinkle with cashew nuts. Serve with lime wedges to squeeze over.

GF | DF | V (use tofu)

Energy	303kcal (1265kJ)
Protein	25.5g
Carbohydrate	17.1g (14.9g sugars)
Fat	13.6g (2.8g sat fat)

CHOPPED TURKISH SALAD WITH CRISPY PITA AND GARLIC SUMAC YOGHURT.

Makes:	2 portions
Prep time:	20 minutes

Crispy pita
1 pita bread, chopped into
    2cm pieces
1 teaspoon olive oil
1 teaspoon sumac

Chopped salad
4 small vine-ripened tomatoes
¼ telegraph cucumber
½ fennel bulb
1 spring onion
2 tablespoons chopped green
    olives (optional)
Seeds from ½ fresh pomegranate
    or ½ cup seedless grapes,
    cut in half
½ cup mixed mint and basil leaves
1 tablespoon extra-virgin olive oil
juice of ½ lemon
½ cup diced cooked lamb
    or chicken (optional)
Good pinch of sumac

Garlic sumac yoghurt
¼ cup unsweetened natural
    yoghurt
1 small clove garlic, minced
¼ teaspoon sumac

This salad goes with so many things, no wonder it's served with just about every dish in Turkey. We've added some crispy pita and a yoghurt dressing to turn it into more than just a side. It's a delicious, filling salad as is, but feel free to add some cooked lamb or chicken to it.

Preheat oven to 180°C. Line an oven tray with baking paper.

1. On lined tray, toss pita bread pieces with olive oil, sumac and a good pinch of flaky sea salt. Spread out in a single layer and bake for 12–15 minutes or until golden and crispy. Set aside to cool.

2. While the pita is baking, prepare salad vegetables – remove seeds from tomatoes and dice; cut cucumber in half lengthways, then use a teaspoon to scoop out the seeds and dice; thinly slice fennel and spring onion.

3. Toss vegetables with all remaining salad ingredients and season to taste with salt and pepper.

4. Mix yoghurt, garlic and sumac together, and season with salt and pepper. Thin with a teaspoon or so of water, if needed.

To serve, divide salad between plates, top with crispy pita and drizzle over yoghurt. Sprinkle more sumac on top.

Tip: Sumac, a dried and ground Middle Eastern berry (you'll find it in the spice section), really adds authentic flavour, but if you can't get it a little lemon zest will do the trick, adding a zesty tartness.

V (omit lamb/chicken)

Energy	345kcal (1443kJ)
Protein	17.2g
Carbohydrate	29.8g (8g sugars)
Fat	16.8g (4.2g sat fat)

RED LENTIL, CHICKPEA AND TOMATO SOUP
WITH HERBS AND CHILLI.

85.

Makes:	4 portions
Prep time:	10 minutes
Cook time:	35 minutes

1 teaspoon olive oil
1 large onion, finely diced
2 cloves garlic, finely chopped
1 teaspoon ground cumin
2 teaspoons smoked paprika
1½ tablespoons chopped thyme
2 teaspoons finely chopped
   rosemary leaves
1½ cups split red lentils, rinsed
   and drained
1 x 400g can chopped or
   crushed tomatoes
1 tablespoon tomato paste
¼ teaspoon chilli flakes
1.5 litres salt-reduced chicken
   or vegetable stock
1–2 cups water
1 x 400g can chickpeas, rinsed
   and drained
Juice of ½–1 lemon
200g baby spinach or chopped
   spinach leaves

To serve
¼ cup finely chopped parsley
¼ cup natural unsweetened
   yoghurt or lite sour cream
   (optional)
2 tablespoons finely grated
   Parmesan cheese (optional)

This warming, humble soup uses mostly pantry staple ingredients and is quick and easy to make.

1. Heat olive oil in a large pot on medium heat. Cook onion and garlic, with a good pinch of salt, for 4–5 minutes until onion is soft. If at any time the onion is sticking on the bottom of the pan and burning, add 2 tablespoons of water, stir and it will unstick.

2. Add cumin, paprika, thyme and rosemary and continue cooking for 1 more minute, being careful not to burn the spices and herbs.

3. Add lentils, canned tomatoes, tomato paste, chilli flakes, stock and water. Cover partially and bring to a simmer. Simmer for about 20 minutes, stirring every now and again, until lentils are tender.

4. Add chickpeas and season with lemon juice, salt and pepper. Continue cooking for 10 more minutes.

5. Bring a kettle of water to the boil. Place spinach in a heatproof bowl and pour over boiling water to cover. Leave for a few minutes then drain well. Squeeze out most of excess water, then finely chop spinach, stir into soup and continue simmering for 1–2 more minutes.

To serve, ladle into bowls and top with parsley, a dollop of yoghurt/sour cream (if using) and a sprinkle of Parmesan (if using).

GF	V	DF (omit yoghurt and Parmesan)	Energy	427kcal (1783kJ)
			Protein	31.5g
			Carbohydrate	53.0g (9.1g sugars)
			Fat	5.8g (1.9g sat fat)

ROAST VEG AND QUINOA SALAD
WITH SPICED NUTS AND FETA.

Makes:	2 portions
Prep time:	15 minutes
Cook time:	25 minutes

2 carrots
1 large or 2 small parsnips
1 medium beetroot
2 teaspoons honey
2 teaspoons olive oil
1 teaspoon finely chopped
    rosemary or thyme
¾ cup cooked quinoa or wild
    rice (or a mix)
2 handfuls leafy greens (e.g.
    spinach, rocket, mesclun)
50g feta, crumbled
3–4 tablespoons chopped
    flat-leaf parsley
1 baby radish or baby beetroot,
    very thinly sliced (optional)
Squeeze of lemon juice
2 teaspoons extra-virgin
    olive oil
¼ cup Savoury Nut Scatter
    (see page 247) or chopped
    roasted cashew nuts

This filling salad is a great way to use up leftover roast vegetables – roast extra with dinner the night before and then just toss everything together on the day. The spiced nuts add amazing flavour, but if you haven't made any just throw in some roasted cashew nuts.

Preheat oven to 200°C. Line an oven tray with baking paper.

1. Peel carrots, cut in half lengthways and slice 1cm–thick. Peel parsnip(s) and cut in half: slice thinner bottom half 1cm–thick; cut upper thicker piece in half lengthways first, then slice 1cm–thick. Peel or scrub beetroot and cut into 2cm chunks.

2. Toss vegetables with honey, olive oil and rosemary/thyme on lined tray. Spread out to a single layer, season with salt and pepper and roast for about 25 minutes or until tender and slightly caramelised.

3. When ready to eat, toss roast vegetables with quinoa/wild rice, greens, feta, parsley, raw baby radish/beetroot (if using), lemon juice, extra-virgin olive oil and a pinch of sea salt. Top with Savoury Nut Scatter/cashew nuts.

GF	V	

Energy	390kcal (1629kJ)
Protein	12.5g
Carbohydrate	37.2g (24.2g sugars)
Fat	19.1g (5.8g sat fat)

Makes:	2 portions
Prep time:	15 minutes
Cook time:	15 minutes

1 medium red or purple kumara
  (250g), scrubbed and cut
  into 2cm chunks
1 tablespoon red wine vinegar
1 teaspoon honey
¼ small red onion, thinly sliced
150g green beans or asparagus,
  trimmed and cut in half
½ punnet cherry tomatoes, cut
  in half
8 pitted black Kalamata olives
1–2 tablespoons chopped
  flat-leaf parsley
1 teaspoon extra-virgin olive oil
100g hot smoked salmon,
  flaked into bite-sized pieces
2 soft- or hard-boiled
  free-range eggs, peeled
  and quartered

Creamy dill dressing
2 tablespoons unsweetened
  natural yoghurt
1 tablespoon mayonnaise
½ teaspoon Dijon or wholegrain
  mustard
Juice of 1 lemon
2 teaspoons chopped fresh dill

Here's a twist on the French classic – with protein from the eggs and salmon, and complex carbohydrates from the kumara, it makes a very filling meal, ideal for brunch, lunch or dinner.

Bring a half kettle of water to the boil. Bring a pot of salted water to the boil.

1. Cook kumara in salted water for about 8 minutes or until just tender. Drain well.

2. In a small bowl, mix red wine vinegar with honey. Add red onion and toss to coat, then set aside to marinate for 10 minutes or so.

3. Place green beans/asparagus in a heatproof bowl and pour over boiling water to cover. Leave for about 5 minutes or until bright green and just tender, then drain and run under cold water to cool.

4. Whisk all creamy dill dressing ingredients together in a small bowl and season to taste with salt and pepper.

5. Toss kumara, green beans/asparagus, tomatoes, olives and parsley together with extra-virgin olive oil and 1 tablespoon of the red wine vinegar marinade (from the onions), and season with salt and cracked black pepper. Gently toss with salmon, egg and drained red onion.

Divide salad between plates and drizzle with creamy dill dressing.

GF   DF (use coconut yoghurt)

Energy	439kcal (1835kJ)
Protein	22.9g
Carbohydrate	41.8g (13g sugars)
Fat	18.7g (4g sat fat)

SUPERFOOD SALAD WITH PAN-FRIED HALLOUMI AND AVOCADO DRESSING.

Makes:	4 portions
Prep time:	25 minutes
Cook time:	20 minutes

Superfood salad
½ cup quinoa (white, red or
   black)
¾ cup water
100–120g curly kale
1 medium beetroot
2 carrots
3 baby radishes
1 cup sauerkraut
½ cup finely chopped parsley
6–8 pitted medjool dates,
   chopped
1 teaspoon extra-virgin olive oil
Juice of ½ lemon

Avocado dressing
Flesh of ½ avocado
Juice of ½ lemon
½ small clove garlic, minced
¼ cup cold water

Halloumi and sunflower seeds
¼ cup sunflower seeds
½ teaspoon olive oil
200g halloumi, cut into 12 slices

This salad is packed to the brim with goodness, with lots of fresh super-nutritious vegetables, a creamy avocado dressing, seeds and quinoa. Topped with some golden pan-fried halloumi, it's delicious and will make you feel great!

1. In a small pot, bring quinoa, water and a good pinch of salt to the boil. As soon as it is boiling, cover with a tight-fitting lid and reduce to low heat to cook for 15 minutes. Turn off heat and leave (still covered) to finish steaming for 5 minutes. Remove lid, fluff up grains with a fork and leave to cool slightly.

2. While quinoa is cooking, prep vegetables. Strip kale leaves from their tough stalks and finely slice; discard stalks. Peel and coarsely grate or shred beetroot; peel and coarsely grate or shred carrots; thinly slice radishes. Place all in a bowl, along with sauerkraut, parsley and dates.

3. Blend all avocado dressing ingredients in a blender until smooth, season to taste with salt and pepper and more lemon juice, if needed. Set aside.

4. Add quinoa to salad bowl, drizzle with extra-virgin olive oil and lemon juice and gently toss to combine. Season to taste with salt and pepper.

5. In a small dry fry-pan, toast sunflower seeds on medium heat for about 2 minutes, moving the pan around frequently, until lightly toasted. Set aside.

6. Heat olive oil in a large non-stick fry-pan on medium heat. Pan-fry halloumi for 1–2 minutes on each side until golden.

To serve, divide salad between plates, top with 3 slices halloumi per portion, drizzle with avocado dressing and scatter with toasted sunflower seeds.

GF | V

Energy	449kcal (1878kJ)
Protein	18.8g
Carbohydrate	46.0g (30.3g sugars)
Fat	21g (10.1g sat fat)

SWEET AND NUTTY TABBOULEH
WITH MEDJOOL DATES AND SPICED NUTS.

93.

Makes:	4 portions
Prep time:	15 minutes
Cook time:	15–20 minutes

1 cup cracked freekeh (also
    sometimes called farik)
    or bulghur wheat

1½ cups water

½ teaspoon salt

Finely grated zest and juice of
    1 lemon

2 teaspoons extra-virgin
    olive oil

1 cup finely chopped flat-leaf
    parsley

1 small or ½ medium red onion,
    finely diced

3–4 vine-ripened tomatoes,
    seeds removed and
    finely diced

½ telegraph cucumber, seeds
    removed and finely diced

6 pitted medjool dates,
    chopped

¼ cup Savoury Nut Scatter
    (see page 247) or chopped
    roasted cashew nuts

We love a good tabbouleh, a super fresh and tasty salad of bulghur wheat or freekeh, parsley and lemon. We've added some finely diced fresh vegetables, dates for a little sweetness and crunchy spiced nuts to make this a meal on its own. Serve as is for a delicious lunch or light dinner, or make it into a more substantial protein-packed meal by adding 100g grilled chicken or meat, or 2–3 slices of pan-fried halloumi and a dollop of hummus.

1. Rinse freekah/bulghur wheat, drain and place in a pot with water and salt and bring to the boil. Cover with a lid, reduce to low heat and cook for 15 minutes or until just tender. Drain any excess liquid and leave to cool.

2. Toss cooked, cooled grains with lemon zest and juice, extra-virgin olive oil, parsley, onion, tomatoes, cucumber and dates and season to taste with salt and pepper. Scatter with nuts just before serving.

DF | V | GF (use quinoa instead of
freekeh/bulghur)

Energy   353kcal (1477kJ)
Protein   12.8g
Carbohydrate   58.6g (28.3g sugars)
Fat   7.8g (1.00g sat fat)

ASIAN NOODLE SALAD
WITH EGG, LEFTOVER CHICKEN OR TOFU.

Makes:	1 portion (but double, triple or quadruple as necessary)
Prep time:	10 minutes

With a few simple ingredients, some leftover protein, and a zesty Asian dressing, you can quickly toss up a very tasty noodle lunch box.

1. Toss all noodle salad ingredients together and place either in a serving bowl or your lunch box (if taking with you).
2. Toss noodles with dressing just before eating.
3. Top with egg, chicken or tofu. Eat up!

Noodle salad
½ cup cooked wholegrain, vegetable-based or rice noodles (e.g. soba, vermicelli, rice stick, quinoa spaghetti, edamame fettuccine, etc.)
½ carrot, peeled and shredded or coarsely grated
½ Lebanese cucumber, halved lengthways, seeds scooped out and sliced
1 baby bok choy, leaves and most of stem thinly sliced
1 spring onion, thinly sliced
¼–½ red chilli, finely chopped (optional)
¼ cup mixture of Asian herbs (e.g. coriander, mint, Vietnamese mint and Thai basil)
1 tablespoon chopped roasted peanuts or cashew nuts
2 tablespoons Asian Dressing (see page 256)

Toppings (choose one of the below)
1 soft or hard-boiled free-range egg, peeled and cut in half
60g cooked shredded chicken
100g cooked and cubed tofu

DF	GF	V

EGG		TOFU		CHICKEN	
Energy	251kcal (1051kJ)	Energy	261kcal (1092kJ)	Energy	289kcal (1206kJ)
Protein	15.5g	Protein	16.4g	Protein	27.8g
Carbohydrate	26.8g (12.1g sugars)	Carbohydrate	27g (12g sugars)	Carbohydrate	26.5g (11.8g sugars)
Fat	9.8g (1.9g sat fat)	Fat	10.3g (1.5g sat fat)	Fat	8.6g (1.7g sat fat)

BROWN RICE VEGGIE BOWL WITH
SMOKED SALMON, SESAME AND PICKLED GINGER.

97.

Makes:	1 portion (but double, triple or quadruple as necessary)
Prep time:	10 minutes

½ cup cooked brown rice
¼ teaspoon soy sauce
2–3 drops sesame oil
¼ capsicum
¼ telegraph or ½ Lebanese cucumber
⅓ cup frozen shelled edamame beans, defrosted

To serve
50g hot-smoked salmon
1–2 teaspoons pickled ginger
½ teaspoon toasted sesame seeds (optional)
1 tablespoon roughly chopped coriander (optional)
1 lemon or lime wedge

This is a good lunch box idea for using up leftover cooked rice and can be served cold or warmed up. You can mix it up by replacing the smoked salmon with 95g canned salmon or tuna, 100g cooked chicken or ¼ avocado.

Bring a half kettle of water to the boil.

1. Season rice to taste with soy sauce and sesame oil. Remove core and seeds from capsicum and thinly slice. Slice cucumber or cut into sticks.

2. Place edamame beans in a small, heatproof bowl and pour over boiling water. Leave for 1–2 minutes before draining. Season with a little salt.

3. To serve, spoon seasoned rice into a bowl and place vegetables and smoked salmon around the outside. Garnish with pickled ginger, sesame seeds and coriander (if using) and serve with lemon/lime wedge to squeeze over just before eating.

Tip: If using leftover cooked rice it is best to heat this (in the microwave is easiest) before eating. Cold cooked rice will keep in an airtight container in the fridge for up to 2 days, or can be frozen in a plastic resealable bag or airtight container.

DF	GF (use GF soy sauce)	V (serve with avocado instead of salmon)

Energy	366kcal (1528kJ)
Protein	23.5g
Carbohydrate	38.0g (2.9g sugars)
Fat	12.5g (2.4g sat fat)

MEDITERRANEAN TUNA AND CHICKPEA SALAD WITH FETA AND PARSLEY.

Makes:	1 portion (but double, triple or quadruple as necessary)
Prep time:	10 minutes

Mediterranean tuna and chickpea salad

1 x 95g can tuna in spring water, drained and flaked

½ x 400g can chickpeas, rinsed and drained

2 tablespoons pitted Kalamata or black olives, cut in half

1 tomato, diced

¼ telegraph or 1 Lebanese cucumber, diced

1 stick celery, thinly sliced

¼ capsicum, core and seeds removed and thinly sliced or diced 1cm

1–2 handfuls shredded lettuce or leafy greens (e.g. baby spinach, baby kale, rocket)

30g feta, crumbled

2 tablespoons finely chopped parsley

Red wine vinaigrette

2 teaspoons extra-virgin olive oil

1 level teaspoon Dijon mustard

2 teaspoons red wine vinegar

1 teaspoon honey

⅛ red onion, finely diced

Packed with sunny Mediterranean flavours, this quick fresh salad is filling and delicious. Chop extra veggies and store in an airtight container in the fridge for round two the next day!

1. Toss all tuna salad ingredients together and place either in a serving bowl or your lunch box (if taking with you).

2. In a small bowl, whisk together all red wine vinaigrette ingredients.

Toss dressing with tuna salad just before eating. Season to taste with salt and freshly ground black pepper. Enjoy your quick and easy lunch!

GF

Energy	444kcal (1858kJ)
Protein	35.3g
Carbohydrate	31.1g (16.0g sugars)
Fat	18.8g (4.8g sat fat)

MIDDLE EASTERN PLATE WITH BOILED EGG, PICKLES, DUKKAH, HUMMUS AND FLATBREAD.

101.

Makes:	1 portion (but double, triple or quadruple as necessary)
Prep time:	10 minutes

¼ red onion, thinly sliced
2 tablespoons red wine vinegar
1 small flatbread or small pita
¼ cup hummus of your choice
    (store-bought or see page 211)
1 soft- or hard-boiled free-range
    egg, peeled
1 tomato, sliced
½ Lebanese cucumber, sliced
3–4 olives or 2 small gherkins
1–2 teaspoons roughly chopped
    flat-leaf parsley
1 teaspoon dukkah or za'atar
¼ teaspoon sumac

When travelling in Turkey, we often ate breakfast similar to this – a light yet substantial assembly of pickles, fresh vegetables, hummus, egg and flatbread. If you like, crumble over 15g feta for extra deliciousness.

1. In a small bowl, toss red onion with vinegar. Set aside to marinate for at least 5 minutes, before draining.

2. Lightly toast or warm flatbread or pita bread (either in oven or toaster).

3. Spoon or spread hummus onto serving plate. Cut boiled egg in half and place on top of hummus, along with pickled onions. Arrange tomato, cucumber and olives/gherkins to the side.

4. Sprinkle parsley, dukkah/za'atar and sumac over hummus and egg. Cut toasted bread into wedges and serve immediately.

Tips:
— If taking to work or on the go, pack the flatbread/pita bread separately to keep it from going soggy and, ideally, toast it fresh at work.
— Sumac, a dried and ground Middle Eastern berry (you'll find it in the spice section), really adds authentic flavour, but if you can't get it a little lemon zest will do the trick, adding a zesty tartness.

DF | V

Energy   351kcal (1467kJ)
Protein   17.6g
Carbohydrate   39g (8.4g sugars)
Fat   12.5g (2.0g sat fat)

SUPER SUSHI
WITH QUINOA SUSHI RICE.

Makes:	4 portions (1 portion = 6 pieces of sushi)
Prep time:	30 minutes
Cook time:	25 minutes

Quinoa sushi rice

½ cup short-grain sushi rice or
   short-grain brown rice
½ cup quinoa (use any colour,
   e.g. white, red or black)
1½ cups water
1 tablespoon Japanese rice vinegar
1 teaspoon mirin (if you don't have
   mirin, use ½ teaspoon sugar)
3 sheets nori (dried seaweed)

To assemble and serve

Your choice of filling (see right)
Soy sauce or tamari
Wasabi
Pickled ginger

This recipe originally featured in an earlier cookbook of mine, *Let's Eat!,* but I had to include it here as well, as sushi is such a great healthy lunch box meal, especially when you use a rice-quinoa mix (this helps bump up the protein and lower the glycaemic index) and keep the fillings super nutritious and fresh.

1. Combine rice, quinoa, water and a good pinch of salt in a pot, cover and bring to the boil. Reduce to lowest heat and simmer, covered, for 15 minutes. Turn off heat and leave to finish steaming, still covered, for a further 8 minutes.

2. Spread cooked rice out on a tray or in a large dish and sprinkle with vinegar and mirin (or sugar). Leave to cool, then mix to distribute the vinegar and mirin through evenly.

3. To roll the sushi, place a sheet of nori on a clean, dry, flat surface (bench or chopping board), making sure the rough side of the nori is facing up. Wet your hands (to avoid sticky fingers) and make a handful of rice (or about one-third of the rice) into a ball. Place in the middle and gently spread it (don't compress it) equally over the nori, creating a layer of rice that covers almost all the nori, except a 2cm margin at the top (you'll see why you need this empty space when you come to rolling the sushi!).

4. Arrange chosen filling along the length of the nori, closest to you. Roll the nori and rice over the filling, enclosing it firmly, then continue rolling with gentle pressure so that the roll is nice and tight. When you get to the 2cm margin at the top, dip your finger in water and wet the strip of nori ever so slightly. Then continue rolling to close the sushi — the damp nori will stick to the rest of the roll. Repeat with remaining nori, quinoa rice and fillings.

5. Use a sharp, clean knife to cut each roll into 8 pieces. Serve with soy sauce/tamari, wasabi and pickled ginger.

DF | V | GF (use GF Tamari)

Tuna mayo and avocado

1 x 185g can tuna in spring water, drained and flaked
2½ tablespoons mayonnaise
2 tablespoons finely diced red onion or 1 thinly sliced
    spring onion (optional)
½ telegraph cucumber or
    1 Lebanese cucumber
Flesh of ½ firm ripe avocado

In a bowl, mash tuna with mayonnaise and red onion/spring onion (if using) and season with a little salt and pepper. Cut cucumber in half, then cut each half into quarters lengthways and scoop out the seeds. Cut each piece into three strips. Slice avocado.

DF	GF	

Energy	345kcal (1442kJ)
Protein	17.5g
Carbohydrate	32.7g (1.3g sugars)
Fat	15.7g (2.8g sat fat)

Salmon cucumber

300g fresh salmon fillet, skin removed and pin-boned
½ telegraph cucumber or 1 Lebanese cucumber

Cut salmon into 1.5cm-wide strips. Cut cucumber in half, then cut each half into quarters lengthways and scoop out the seeds. Cut each piece into three strips.

DF	GF	

Energy	380kcal (1589kJ)
Protein	18.8g
Carbohydrate	32.1 (0.8g sugars)
Fat	19.6g (5.0g sat fat)

Egg omelette and vegetables

3 free-range eggs
1 teaspoon sesame oil
½ red capsicum
½ telegraph cucumber or
    1 Lebanese cucumber
1 carrot
Flesh of ½ firm ripe avocado

Whisk eggs together and season with a little salt. Heat sesame oil in a small non-stick fry-pan on medium heat. Pour in eggs and cook for about 2–3 minutes, allowing to set as an omelette. Once omelette is cooked, remove from pan, allow to cool, then slice. Core and thinly slice capsicum. Cut cucumber in half, then cut each half into quarters lengthways and scoop out the seeds. Cut each piece into three strips. Peel carrot and cut into fine matchsticks. Slice avocado.

DF	GF	V	

Energy	291kcal (1215kJ)
Protein	10.7g
Carbohydrate	33.7g (2.3g sugars)
Fat	12.0g (1.9g sat fat)

Teriyaki chicken and capsicum

½ teaspoon oil
200g boneless, skinless chicken thighs
    (about 2 chicken thighs), cut into 1cm-thick strips
1 tablespoon soy sauce or tamari
1 tablespoon honey
½ teaspoon sesame oil
1 red capsicum
½ telegraph or 1 Lebanese cucumber

Pat chicken dry with paper towels. Heat oil in a small fry-pan on medium heat and cook chicken for about 3 minutes or until just cooked through. Mix soy sauce/tamari, honey and sesame oil in a small bowl and add to pan with the chicken – bring to a bubble and spoon glaze over chicken, tossing well to coat. Core and thinly slice capsicum. Cut cucumber in half, then cut each half into quarters lengthways and scoop out the seeds. Cut each piece into three strips.

DF	GF (use GF Tamari)	

Energy	265kcal (1108kJ)
Protein	15.4g
Carbohydrate	37.5g (6.0g sugars)
Fat	5.6g (1.0g sat fat)

Makes:	6 portions (1 portion = 2 fritartlets)
Prep time:	15 minutes
Cook time:	20–25 minutes

2 teaspoons olive oil or butter,
   for greasing
1 teaspoon olive oil or butter
2–3 spring onions, thinly sliced
   (reserve about 2 tablespoons
   of thinly sliced green part)
2 teaspoons chopped thyme or
   rosemary
2 rashers lean (e.g. shoulder or
   middle) bacon, diced or 100g
   hot smoked salmon
3–4 cups thinly sliced spinach,
   silverbeet or kale leaves
8 free-range eggs
¼ cup natural unsweetened
   Greek yoghurt
½ teaspoon salt
2 cups diced roast butternut
   or pumpkin
6 cherry tomatoes, cut in half
50g feta

To serve
Side salad
Tomato chutney (optional)

These are frittatas in little tart form – they make a delicious lunch with a salad and some chutney. Choose from either bacon or smoked salmon flavour.

Preheat oven to 180°C and grease a 12-hole medium or large muffin tin with olive oil/butter. Bring a half kettle of water to the boil.

1. Heat olive oil/butter in a small fry-pan on medium heat. Cook spring onion, thyme/rosemary and bacon (if using) for a few minutes. Place spinach in a heatproof bowl and pour over boiling water to cover. Leave for about 2 minutes then drain well, squeeze out as much excess water as you can, and finely chop.

2. In a large bowl, whisk eggs with yoghurt, spinach, spring onion mixture and salt until well combined. Pour into a jug (this will make it much easier to pour into muffin tins).

3. Divide mixture equally between the muffin tin holes, being careful not to overfill – it should come up no more than three-quarters of the way. Top each with some pumpkin, smoked salmon (if using instead of bacon), and a cherry tomato half. Crumble feta on top and sprinkle with reserved green spring onion. Grind over black pepper. Bake for 18–20 minutes until egg is set. Allow to cool in the tin for a few minutes before using a knife to cut around and separate from the edges of the muffin tin and lift them out.

Serve warm (see tip) or cold with a side salad and, if you like, a teaspoon of tomato chutney on the side. If not eating immediately, allow to cool before storing in an airtight container in the fridge where they'll keep for up to 3 days.

Tips:
— This recipe can easily be halved if you
   only want to make 6 fritartlets (3 portions).
— Reheat in the microwave for 30 seconds or
   in a 150°C oven for 5 minutes.

GF

Energy	207kcal (865kJ)
Protein	16.2g
Carbohydrate	5.8g (3.1g sugars)
Fat	12.9g (4.3g sat fat)

RAINBOW WRAPS.

Wrap a whole lot of delicious nutritious ingredients
up in collard green leaves for a super fresh and
healthy lunch box. If you can't get collard greens
(a big leafy green vegetable), you could just serve
the fillings with some iceberg lettuce leaves and
stuff them to make rainbow 'cups', or even
use wholemeal wraps.

Makes:	1 portion
Prep time:	20 minutes
Cook time:	5 minutes

4 collard green leaves or 2 small
    wholemeal wraps
Your choice of filling (see over page)

1. Bring a half kettle of water to the boil. If using collard green wraps, cut each leaf in half down either side of the tough inner stem. Discard the stems. Place leaves in a large heatproof bowl and pour over boiling water to cover. Leave for 30–60 seconds, then drain off hot water. Pour over cold water and add some ice cubes to cool the leaves down. This process makes the leaves flexible for folding and tender for eating. Drain and pat leaves dry with paper towels. If not using immediately, keep in fridge for up to 2 days lightly wrapped in paper towels.

2. To assemble a wrap, place two leaves together on a clean flat surface such as a chopping board, as if you're making a whole leaf again, overlapping in the middle by about 1cm. Arrange filling across the bottom centre of the leaf (going across the cut line). Fold the sides of the leaves in towards the centre, followed by the bottom, so your fillings are enclosed. Then, using your hands to keep the sides of the leaf tucked in, roll the wrap from the bottom like you're folding a burrito. Repeat with remaining wraps.

3. With a serrated knife, carefully slice each wrap in half to serve. Or, if you're going to travel with your wrap, leave it whole and cut it when ready to eat.

PRAWN OR CHICKEN, AVOCADO AND MANGO
WITH CHILLI AND LIME DIPPING SAUCE.

111.

Per portion	**(4 collard green wraps or 2 small wholemeal wraps)**

½ mango, peeled and cut into matchsticks

8 cooked and shelled prawns, diced or split in half lengthways, or 100g cooked chicken

½ Lebanese cucumber, seeds removed and cut into batons

Flesh of ¼ firm ripe avocado, cut into 4 slices

½ red capsicum, cored and thinly sliced

¼ cup mint leaves or coriander

Chilli and lime dipping sauce

Juice of 1 lime

1½ teaspoons sweet chilli sauce (store-bought or see page 258)

½ teaspoon fish or soy sauce

1. Divide mango, prawns/chicken, cucumber, avocado, capsicum and mint/coriander in the centre of each wrap, and follow wrapping instructions on previous page.

2. To make dipping sauce, in a small bowl, mix all ingredients together.

DF   GF (use collard greens or lettuce cups)

Energy	346kcal (1448kJ)
Protein	21.8g
Carbohydrate	30.3g (22.5g sugars)
Fat	13.9g (2.1g sat fat)

HALLOUMI, HUMMUS AND SUPERFOOD SALAD.

Per portion: (4 collard green wraps or 2 small wholemeal wraps)

½ teaspoon olive oil
40–50g halloumi, cut into
    4 thick slices
¼ cup hummus (store-bought
    or see page 211)
1 cup Superfood Salad
    (see page 90)

1. Heat olive oil in a non-stick fry-pan on medium heat and pan-fry halloumi for 1–2 minutes on both sides until golden.

2. Place a piece of halloumi in the centre of each wrap, spread with hummus and top with superfood salad.

V   GF (use collard greens or lettuce cups)

Energy	355kcal (1485kJ)
Protein	16.5g
Carbohydrate	25.6g (16.8g sugars)
Fat	19.8g (9.3g sat fat)

chapter three—

fast
dinners

- The dinners in this section are *around 30 minutes or less* from start to finish. Get dinner on the table even faster by doing a little prep in advance. If your meat and chicken is pre-portioned, grab it from the freezer and leave it in the fridge to defrost over the day, and if you have 10 spare minutes in the morning do some vegetable prep – you'll be super thankful for it at the end of a busy day!

- *Plan your meals.* If you don't get the Fresh Start bag, make sure you plan your meals for the week to avoid last-minute dashes to the shops and disappointment when you're missing that one ingredient you need.

- *Snack on fresh vegetable sticks while you prepare dinner.* This will stop you from constantly picking (at the grated cheese!), get even more vegetables into your day, and avoid you being too ravenous at dinner time; but you'll still be hungry enough to enjoy your dinner.

- *Eat at the table, sitting down and enjoy your dinner over at least 15–20 minutes.* It takes this amount of time for the hormone leptin to kick in and tell your brain you're full. *Chew each mouthful at least 20 times* and put your knife and fork down in between each bite. Soon it will all become second nature!

- *If you're cooking for the rest of the family too, get them involved* in some of the meal prep. Little ones LOVE helping with stirring or mixing (and from my experience are far more likely to eat the end result if they've helped), and older kids can even prep or cook part of the meal a few times a week.

Makes:	4 portions
Prep time:	20 minutes
Cook time:	15 minutes

Aztec steak and corn
550g lean sirloin, rump or
    eye fillet beef steaks (or lamb
    or venison loin), at room
    temperature
4 corn cobs, husks and silk
    removed
3 teaspoons Mexican Seasoning
    (store-bought or see page 256)
2 teaspoons oil

Garden salsa
¼ red onion
2 Lebanese cucumbers or
    ½ telegraph cucumber
1 punnet cherry tomatoes
1 courgette

To serve
¾ cup Chimichurri
    (see page 257)

If you're wanting to use the BBQ to cook your steak and corn, preheat it to high.

1. Start by making the Chimichurri.
2. Rub corn with 1 teaspoon of the oil and sprinkle with 1½ teaspoons of the Mexican Seasoning. Rub steaks with the remaining 1½ teaspoons Mexican Seasoning.
3. Heat remaining 1 teaspoon of oil in a large fry-pan on high heat. Cook steaks for about 2 minutes on each side (for medium-rare, depending on thickness, or until done to your liking), and corn cobs for 3–4 minutes on each side, until a little charred. Alternatively, cook steaks and corn on the BBQ. Cover cooked steaks with foil and leave to rest for 5–10 minutes before slicing against the grain.
4. While steak and corn are cooking and resting, make the salsa. Finely dice red onion; cut cucumber(s) in half, scoop out seeds with a teaspoon and dice flesh; cut cherry tomatoes into quarters; finely dice courgette and add all to a bowl. Toss with half of the Chimichurri.

To serve, divide corn, steak and salsa between plates and spoon remaining Chimichurri over steak and corn.

DF   GF

Energy	445kcal (1859kJ)
Protein	36.2g
Carbohydrate	21.5g (5.8g sugars)
Fat	22.9g (6.0g sat fat)

BROWN RICE NASI GORENG WITH CHICKEN, TOFU OR PRAWNS, VEGETABLES AND A FRIED EGG.

123.

Makes:	4 portions
Prep time:	15 minutes
Cook time:	20 minutes

Fried eggs
1 teaspoon sesame oil
4 free-range eggs

Nasi goreng
300g chicken breast, cut into thin strips, or 400g raw shelled prawns (defrosted if frozen), or 400g cubed firm tofu, or a mix of any
1½ teaspoons curry powder
1 teaspoon sesame oil
3 spring onions, white part only (reserve green part), thinly sliced
50g store-bought nasi goreng paste (e.g. Asian Home Gourmet)
1½ tablespoons soy sauce
2¼ teaspoons honey
2 teaspoons sweet chilli sauce (store-bought or see page 258)
2 cups cooked brown or wild rice (see tip)
1 cup frozen peas, defrosted
3–4 cups finely chopped vegetables such as broccoli, cauliflower and/or cabbage
1 carrot, peeled and finely diced

To serve
2 cups mung bean sprouts or chopped lettuce
Reserved spring onion greens, thinly sliced
Chopped coriander
2 red chillies, thinly sliced
1 lemon, cut into wedges

Our nasi goreng, or Indonesian fried rice, has had a healthy makeover by using brown rice and loads more vegetables. If you like, for a super convenient meal, just use 3½–4 cups frozen mixed vegetables in place of the fresh broccoli, carrot and peas.

1. For the fried eggs, heat sesame oil in a medium-large non-stick fry-pan on medium heat. Crack in eggs, one by one, and cook for about 3 minutes or until cooked to your liking. Set aside and keep warm.

2. To make nasi goreng, pat chicken/prawns/tofu dry with paper towels. Dust in curry powder and a good pinch of salt. Heat sesame oil in a wok or your largest (preferably non-stick) fry-pan on medium-high heat. Add chicken/prawns/tofu and white part of spring onion and cook, stirring often, for 4–5 minutes until browned. Add nasi goreng paste and continue cooking for 1–2 more minutes until fragrant. Set aside on a plate, keep pan on the heat.

3. Mix soy sauce, honey and sweet chilli sauce in a bowl.

4. Add cooked rice, vegetables, and soy sauce mixture to the pan, and cook, stirring, for 4–5 minutes or until vegetables are just tender. Add back chicken/prawn/tofu mixture and toss everything together for a further 1–2 minutes until combined. Season to taste with more soy sauce (if needed) and freshly ground black pepper.

5. To serve, spoon nasi goreng onto plates. Top with mung bean sprouts/lettuce, spring onion greens, coriander, chilli and a fried egg. Serve with a lemon wedge to squeeze over just before eating.

Tip: It's best to use leftover cooked rice that's been stored in the fridge overnight as it will be drier and you'll end up with a fluffier fried rice. However, if you haven't got any leftover rice, just cook some fresh, spread out in a dish and leave to cool in the fridge or freezer before using. ⅔ cup of uncooked rice will yield 2 cups of cooked rice.

DF   GF (check nasi goreng paste and use GF soy sauce)

CHICKEN		TOFU		PRAWN	
Energy	432cal (1807kJ)	Energy	433kcal (1810kJ)	Energy	439kcal (1833kJ)
Protein	33.5g	Protein	24.8g	Protein	37.2g
Carbohydrate	42.7g (9.8g sugars)	Carbohydrate	43.9g (10.3g sugars)	Carbohydrate	42.7g (9.8g sugars)
Fat	12.8g (2.7g sat fat)	Fat	16.0g (2.8g sat fat)	Fat	11.8g (2.3g sat fat)

CHICKEN AND EGGPLANT PARMIGIANA WITH ROSEMARY ROASTED KUMARA.

Makes:	4 portions
Prep time:	20 minutes
Cook time:	30 minutes

Rosemary roasted kumara
400g red, gold or orange
   kumara, skin left on,
   scrubbed and cut into
   1–2cm cubes
1½ teaspoons olive oil
2 teaspoons rosemary leaves

Parmigiana
550g (about 2 large) skinless
   chicken breasts
1 teaspoon oil
1 x 400g can crushed tomatoes
2 tablespoons tomato paste
½ teaspoon dried mixed herbs
¼ teaspoon chilli flakes
   (optional)
1 large eggplant, cut into
   1cm slices
2 teaspoons olive oil,
   for brushing
½ cup grated mozzarella
   cheese
2 tablespoons finely grated
   Parmesan cheese

To serve
Fresh basil leaves, to garnish
Green Salad (see page 251) or
Sautéed Veggies (see page 248)

We love this simple Italian dish of grilled chicken, eggplant, rich tomato sauce and gooey melted mozzarella. Best served simply with a green salad or sautéed veggies.

Preheat oven to 200°C and line an oven tray with baking paper.

1. Toss kumara with olive oil and rosemary on lined oven tray and season with salt and pepper. Roast for about 15 minutes until golden, turning once during cooking.

2. Pat chicken breasts dry with paper towels and cut horizontally into thin steaks; to do this, lay one hand flat on top of a chicken breast on a chopping board and use a large sharp knife in the other hand to carefully and evenly slice through horizontally, keeping equal thickness on either side as best as you can. Season each piece with salt. Heat oil in a large fry-pan. Brown chicken steaks for 1 minute on each side (do not cook all the way through). Set aside.

3. Tip crushed tomatoes into fry-pan chicken was cooked in, stir in tomato paste, dried herbs and chilli flakes (if using), and simmer, stirring frequently, on medium heat for about 8 minutes or until sauce has thickened. Season to taste with salt and pepper and set aside.

4. Once kumara is cooked, transfer to a bowl, keep warm and switch oven to grill. Arrange eggplant on same lined tray, brush (or spray) lightly with olive oil and season with salt. Grill for 6–8 minutes, turning halfway through cooking, until soft and lightly browned. Transfer to a plate (but keep lined tray).

5. Place chicken steaks on lined tray and top with eggplant slices, dividing equally. Spread with tomato sauce then sprinkle with mozzarella and Parmesan. Grill for 5–6 minutes or until chicken is cooked through and cheese is melted and bubbly.

6. Garnish parmigiana with basil and serve with roasted kumara and green salad or sautéed veggies.

GF

Energy	435kcal (1820kJ)
Protein	40.7g
Carbohydrate	32.1g (9.8g sugars)
Fat	14.7g (4.4g sat fat)

Makes:	4 portions
Prep time:	20 minutes
Cook time:	30 minutes

500g boneless, skinless chicken
   thighs, cut into quarters
1 teaspoon olive oil
2 slices lean shoulder or mid-eye
   bacon, rind removed, diced
250g punnet button mushrooms,
   cut into quarters
1 onion, thinly sliced
1 red capsicum, cored and thinly
   sliced
2 sticks celery or 1 fennel bulb,
   diced
2 cloves garlic, chopped
1½ tablespoons chopped rosemary
   leaves
1 teaspoon dried oregano or mixed
   herbs
100ml dry white wine, verjuice or
   chicken stock
1 x 400g can crushed tomatoes
1 tablespoon tomato paste
1 tablespoon red wine vinegar
8–10 pitted black or green olives,
   cut in half
¼ cup chopped flat-leaf parsley

To serve
Cauliflower Parsley Mash
   (see page 234)
Sautéed Veggies (see page 248)

A warming, comforting stew of chicken, mushrooms, celery and a bit of bacon for extra flavour. It's delicious served with a creamy cauliflower mash to soak up all the juices, and steamed vegetables.

1. Pat chicken dry with paper towels. Heat ½ teaspoon of the olive oil in a large fry-pan on medium-high heat. Season chicken with salt and pan-fry in two batches, adding remaining oil in between, for 1–2 minutes on each side until golden brown (it does not have to be cooked all the way through). Set chicken aside on a plate and keep pan on the heat.

2. Add bacon, mushrooms, onion, capsicum and celery/ fennel to pan, with a good pinch of salt, and cook for about 6 minutes, until vegetables are soft. Add garlic, rosemary and dried herbs, and continue cooking for 2 minutes or so.

3. Add wine/verjuice/stock and bring to the boil for a minute or two, then stir in crushed tomatoes, tomato paste, red wine vinegar, browned chicken and olives. Simmer for 8–10 minutes until sauce has slightly thickened and chicken is cooked through. Season to taste with salt and pepper and scatter parsley on top.

Serve with cauliflower parsley mash and sautéed veggies.

DF | GF

Energy	436kcal (1821kJ)
Protein	37.9g
Carbohydrate	26.9g (13.7g sugars)
Fat	15.1g (3.7g sat fat)

CHICKEN TIKKA SKEWERS WITH RAITA AND CAULIFLOWER PILAF.

Makes:	4 portions
Prep time:	30 minutes
Cook time:	20 minutes

8 bamboo or metal skewers (if using bamboo, soak skewers in water before cooking)

Chicken tikka skewers
550g lean chicken mince
¾ teaspoon salt
50g Tandoori Paste (store-bought or see page 256)
¼ cup dried breadcrumbs or ground almonds
2 teaspoons oil

Raita
1 Lebanese or ¼ telegraph cucumber
⅔ cup unsweetened natural yoghurt
1–2 tablespoons finely chopped mint leaves

Cauliflower pilaf
1 teaspoon oil
1 onion, diced
1 teaspoon garam masala
½ teaspoon each ground cumin and ground coriander
¼ cup sultanas
6–7 cups coarsely grated or finely chopped cauliflower (from 1 head cauliflower)
½ cup chicken stock
1 bag (120–150g) baby spinach, chopped

To serve
¼ cup chopped mint leaves or coriander
1 lemon, cut into wedges

The beautiful fragrant spices used in Indian cooking give so much flavour, making it easy to create a flavour-packed meal that's lean and healthy. If you like, skip the skewers and make chicken tikka meatballs!

Preheat oven to 200°C. Line an oven tray with baking paper.

1. Place all chicken tikka skewers ingredients, except oil, in a bowl and use clean hands to mix well. If you have time, set mixture aside in the fridge to firm up a little before shaping onto skewers.

2. To make raita, cut cucumber in half lengthways, then use a teaspoon to scoop out the seeds. Grate cucumber straight onto a clean tea towel, then wring to squeeze out excess moisture. In a bowl, mix cucumber with yoghurt and mint, season with salt and pepper and set aside.

3. Roughly divide chicken mixture into eight and shape mixture around each skewer, like a long meatball on a stick. Heat 1 teaspoon of the oil in a large non-stick fry-pan on medium-high heat. Brown skewers in two batches, adding remaining oil in between, for 2 minutes on each side, then place on oven tray and transfer to oven to finish cooking for 5 minutes. Wash out pan to cook pilaf.

4. For the pilaf, heat oil on medium heat. Cook onion until starting to turn golden, add spices and sultanas and continue cooking for a further minute. Add cauliflower and chicken stock and bring to a simmer and steam for 2–3 minutes or until cauliflower is just tender, but still has texture/bite, and all the liquid has evaporated. Toss through spinach and season to taste with salt and pepper.

To serve, divide cauliflower pilaf, skewers and raita between plates. Sprinkle with mint/coriander and serve with lemon wedges to squeeze over just before eating.

DF (use coconut yoghurt) | GF (use ground almonds)

Energy	380kcal (1589kJ)
Protein	32.6g
Carbohydrate	21.8g (18.8g sugars)
Fat	17.2g (3.3g sat fat)

GADO GADO SALAD WITH SPICED TOFU, EGG AND PEANUT SATAY SAUCE.

131.

Makes:	**4 portions**
Prep time:	**20 minutes**
Cook time:	**5 minutes**

Salad
250g kumara or potato,
    scrubbed (leave skin
    on), cut into 2cm cubes
½ telegraph cucumber
1 green/unripe mango
¼–½ green cabbage
4 baby radishes
200g green beans
2 cups mung bean sprouts

Peanut satay sauce
½ cup peanut butter (up to
    you whether it's smooth
    or crunchy)
2 teaspoons soy sauce
1½ teaspoons fish sauce
2 tablespoons lime or
    lemon juice
1½ tablespoons tamarind paste
    or purée
2 tablespoons sweet chilli sauce
    (store-bought or see page 258)
⅓ cup water

Spiced tofu
300g–400g firm tofu cut into
    1–2cm cubes or (chicken
    breast, cut into strips)
1½ teaspoons curry powder
1 teaspoon sesame oil

To serve
2 soft- or hard-boiled free-range
    eggs, peeled and cut in half
½ cup chopped coriander
Lime or lemon wedges

This salad has it all – loads of crunchy fresh vegetables, golden-spiced and fried tofu (however, if you like, use strips of chicken breast instead), kumara or potato, hard-boiled egg and an amaaazing peanut satay sauce to finish it all off!

Bring a half kettle of water to the boil.

1. Place kumara/potato in a pot of salted water and bring to the boil. Cook for about 8 minutes until just tender. Drain.

2. While kumara is cooking, prepare the other salad ingredients – cut cucumber in half lengthways, scoop out seeds using a teaspoon, then slice into half-moons; peel and thinly slice mango; finely shred cabbage until you have 4 cups worth; thinly slice radishes; trim green beans, place in a heatproof bowl, pour over boiling water and leave for 1–2 minutes before draining and running under cold water. Set all aside with mung bean sprouts.

3. In a small pot, mix all peanut satay sauce ingredients together and heat gently. Stir in a few tablespoons more water if the sauce seems too thick.

4. Pat tofu/chicken dry with paper towels and toss with curry powder and a good pinch of salt. Heat sesame oil in a large non-stick fry-pan. Add tofu/chicken and cook for 3–4 minutes until golden all over.

5. Divide salad ingredients and kumara/potato between serving plates or bowls, top with tofu/chicken and half an egg. Drizzle with satay sauce, scatter with coriander and serve with lime or lemon wedges to squeeze over just before eating.

MOROCCAN LAMB SALAD
WITH ROAST CARROTS AND GRAPE BULGHUR.

Makes:	4 portions
Prep time:	25 minutes
Cook time:	30 minutes

Harissa lamb
550g lean lamb loin, leg steaks or
 rump, or tenderloins
2 tablespoons Harissa Paste
 (store-bought or see page 257)
1 teaspoon olive oil

Roast carrots
400–500g baby carrots, trimmed
 (or large carrots cut into batons)
1½ teaspoons olive oil
1½ teaspoons honey
1½ teaspoons sumac (optional)

Grape bulghur
1 teaspoon olive oil
2 shallots or 1 small onion,
 finely diced
½ teaspoon each ground allspice
 and ground cinnamon
½ cup dried bulghur wheat
¾ cup chicken stock
1½ cups frozen peas, edamame
 or broad beans, defrosted
¼ cup chopped flat-leaf parsley
¼ cup chopped coriander or mint
1 cup seedless grapes, cut in half,
 or 3 pitted medjool dates,
 finely chopped
¼ cup lightly toasted flaked
 almonds
Zest and juice of ½ lemon

To serve
¼ cup unsweetened natural
 yoghurt
1½–2 teaspoons Harissa Paste
 (store-bought or see page 257)

With flavours of the Middle East and North Africa, this is one flavour-packed meal.

Preheat oven to 200°C. Line an oven tray with baking paper.

1. Pat lamb dry with paper towels and coat with harissa paste. Leave to marinate at room temp while you prepare the rest of the meal. Alternatively leave to marinate in the fridge for a few hours or overnight.

2. Toss carrots with olive oil, honey and sumac (if using) on lined oven tray and season with salt and pepper. Spread out into a single layer and roast, tossing once during cooking, for about 20 minutes until tender and lightly caramelised.

3. For the bulghur, heat olive oil in a medium pot on low-medium heat. Cook shallot/onion, with a good pinch of salt, for 1-2 minutes until soft and fragrant. If at any time the onion/shallot is sticking to the bottom of the pan and burning, add a tablespoon of water, stir and it should unstick. Add allspice, cinnamon and bulghur and toss to coat in the shallot/onion and spices, then add stock. Bring to the boil, then cover with a tight-fitting lid, reduce to low heat and cook for 10 minutes or until bulghur is tender. Turn off heat and leave lid on to finish steaming bulghur for a few minutes before fluffing up with a fork.

4. To cook the lamb, heat olive oil in a large fry-pan on medium-high heat. Season lamb with salt and cook for about 2-3 minutes on each side for medium-rare, or until done to your liking (note: cook times will also depend on the thickness of the cut you use. If using lamb rump, you'll need to finish cooking lamb in the oven for 5-6 minutes as it is thicker). Cover and set aside to rest for 5-10 minutes before slicing against the grain.

5. When bulghur is cooked, toss with roast carrots, peas/edamame/broad beans, fresh herbs, grapes/dates, almonds and lemon zest and juice. Season to taste with salt and pepper. Mix yoghurt with harissa paste and any juices from the resting lamb.

To serve, divide bulghur salad and lamb between plates and serve with a dollop of harissa yoghurt.

DF (use coconut yoghurt)

Energy	447kcal (1868kJ)
Protein	36.6g
Carbohydrate	30.9g (17.5g sugars)
Fat	17.7g (4.8g sat fat)

MASALA LAMB, SWEET POTATOES, PEAS AND GREEN BEANS WITH MINT YOGHURT.

135.

Makes:	4 portions
Prep time:	15 minutes
Cook time:	15 minutes

Masala lamb

550g lean lamb loin, leg steaks
    or rump, or tenderloins
1 teaspoon garam masala
½ teaspoon each ground
    coriander and ground cumin
1 teaspoon oil

**Masala sweet potatoes, peas
and green beans**

400g kumara and/or potatoes,
    scrubbed (leave skin on),
    diced 2cm
1 teaspoon oil
1 large red onion, diced
1 teaspoon mustard seeds
1½ teaspoons curry powder
2 cups frozen peas
300g green beans, trimmed
    and cut in half
4 handfuls chopped spinach
    or silverbeet
Squeeze of lemon juice

Mint yoghurt

½ cup unsweetened natural
    yoghurt
2 tablespoons finely chopped
    mint leaves
Juice of ½ lemon

Using half peas and beans, and half potatoes, bumps up the veg content and lightens up the base for this simple meal of Indian-spiced lamb with a fresh mint yoghurt dressing.

If using lamb rump, preheat oven to 200°C.

1. Boil kumara/potatoes in a pot of well-salted water for 8–10 minutes or until just tender.

2. Pat lamb dry with paper towels, season with salt and coat with spices. Heat oil in a large fry-pan on medium-high heat. Sear lamb for 2–3 minutes on each side until cooked medium-rare (or to your liking). If using lamb rump, you'll need to finish cooking the lamb in the oven for 5–6 more minutes as it is thicker. Once cooked, leave to rest for 5–10 minutes before slicing against the grain. Wipe out fry-pan.

3. For the masala sweet potatoes, heat oil in fry-pan on medium heat. Cook onion, with a good pinch of salt, for a few minutes until soft. Add mustard seeds and curry powder and continue cooking for a further minute until fragrant. Turn off heat.

4. When kumara/potatoes are almost done, but have a couple more minutes of cooking to go, add peas and green beans to the boiling water to lightly cook. Drain all the veggies very well, then tip into spiced onion mixture, along with spinach/silverbeet, and toss everything together until greens have wilted. Season to taste with salt, pepper and a squeeze of lemon juice.

5. Mix yoghurt, mint and lemon juice together in a bowl and season with salt.

To serve, divide kumara/potatoes, vegetables and lamb between plates and drizzle with mint yoghurt.

GF | DF (use coconut yoghurt)

Energy	385kcal (1610kJ)
Protein	36.6g
Carbohydrate	31g (15.9g sugars)
Fat	11.1g (3.9g sat fat)

136. LAMB AND LENTIL MOUSSAKA WITH MIDDLE EASTERN SPICES.

Makes:	4 portions
Prep time:	20 minutes
Cook time:	30 minutes

Eggplant layers

1 large eggplant, cut into
0.5cm-thick slices
2 teaspoons olive oil, for
brushing

Lamb and lentil filling

1 teaspoon olive oil
500g lean ground lamb
¼ teaspoon ground cinnamon
Pinch of ground or grated
nutmeg
1½ teaspoons each ground
cumin, ground coriander,
smoked paprika and dried
mixed herbs
1 red onion, diced
1 clove garlic, finely chopped
1 carrot, peeled and grated
1 courgette, grated
1 x 400g can brown lentils,
rinsed and drained
1 x 400g can chopped tomatoes
2 tablespoons tomato paste
1 tablespoon Worcestershire
sauce

Topping

2 free-range eggs
1 cup natural unsweetened
Greek yoghurt
80–100g soft feta, crumbled
2 tablespoons grated Parmesan
cheese

To serve

Green Salad (see page 251) or
Sautéed Veggies (see page 248)

On their own lentils can be boring, but given some love, with the addition of beautiful spices and paired with lamb mince, they really add to this classic Greek dish. In typical Fresh Start style, we've snuck in extra vegetables and lightened up the topping but it's still creamy and delicious.

Preheat oven grill to high. Line an oven tray with baking paper. Set aside a medium baking dish (measuring about 23 x 23cm or 18 x 27cm, or similar).

1. Place eggplant slices on lined oven tray, brush (or spray) with olive oil and season with salt and pepper. Arrange in a single layer (overlapping slightly is fine) and grill, on upper oven rack, for 4–5 minutes on each side, until softened and starting to brown. Once finished, preheat oven to 200°C bake.

2. While eggplant is grilling, heat oil in a large fry-pan on medium-high heat. Add lamb, spices, dried herbs, and a good pinch of salt, and cook for 3–4 minutes until browned, breaking up mince with a wooden spoon as it cooks. Add onion and garlic and continue cooking for a further 3–4 minutes or until onion is soft.

3. Add carrot and courgette to lamb, and cook for 3 minutes, stirring occasionally, until softened. Stir through lentils, tomatoes, tomato paste and Worcestershire sauce. Simmer on high heat for 5–6 minutes, until all liquid is absorbed. Season to taste with salt and pepper.

4. In a bowl, use a fork to whisk together eggs, yoghurt and feta. Season well with pepper and set aside.

5. Spoon half of the lamb mixture into the base of the baking dish. Arrange half the eggplant slices on top. Repeat with remaining lamb mixture and eggplant. Top with feta mixture, lightly spreading out. Sprinkle with Parmesan. Bake for 15–20 minutes, until bubbly and golden. Remove from oven to rest for 5–10 minutes before cutting into portions.

Serve with a green salad or sautéed veggies.

GF (use GF Worcestershire sauce)

Energy	449kcal (1878kJ)
Protein	44.3g
Carbohydrate	24.5g (13.1g sugars)
Fat	17.9g (7.4g sat fat)

LEMON HONEY PORK WITH KUMARA FETA CRUSH AND APPLE FENNEL SALAD.

139.

Makes:	4 portions
Prep time:	20 minutes
Cook time:	25 minutes

Kumara feta crush

400g red kumara scrubbed
    (leave skin on), diced 2cm
1½ teaspoons olive oil
¼ red onion, finely diced
2 tablespoons chopped parsley
50g feta

Lemon honey pork

1 clove garlic, finely chopped
Zest of ½ lemon
Juice of ¼ lemon
½ teaspoon each lemon pepper
    and paprika
1 teaspoon wholegrain mustard
1 teaspoon ground fennel seeds
    or ground coriander
550g lean pork fillet or sirloin
    steaks, trimmed of excess fat
2 teaspoons olive oil
2 teaspoons honey

Apple fennel salad

1½ teaspoons extra-virgin
    olive oil
3 teaspoons vinegar (e.g. red
    wine, white wine, apple cider)
1–2 teaspoons Dijon or
    wholegrain mustard
1 teaspoon honey
Juice of ¼ lemon
4–5 tablespoons unsweetened
    natural yoghurt
1 cos lettuce
1 red or green apple
1 fennel bulb
2 carrots

We love this meal – pork, kumara, apple and fennel go so well together! Use a lean cut of pork such as fillet or sirloin steaks.

Preheat oven to 200°C. Line an oven tray with baking paper. Preheat BBQ grill or hotplate to medium-high (if using).

1. Toss kumara with olive oil on lined tray and season with salt and pepper. Spread out into a single layer and roast for about 20 minutes or until golden and tender.

2. Place all lemon honey pork ingredients – except the oil and honey – in a bowl and toss to coat pork. Season with salt and pepper, and set aside to marinate.

3. Meanwhile, make the apple and fennel salad. In a small bowl, whisk together extra-virgin olive oil, vinegar, mustard, honey, lemon juice and yoghurt. Roughly chop cos lettuce; cut apple into quarters, remove and discard core, then thinly slice; discard outer layer of fennel bulb and very thinly slice the white part; peel and shred or coarsely grate carrots. Add all to a large bowl with three-quarters of the dressing (reserve the rest for serving) and toss to combine. Season to taste with salt and pepper.

4. Heat olive oil in a large fry-pan on medium-high heat. Cook pork for 3–4 minutes on each side until just cooked through. Turn off the heat and drizzle honey over pork. Quickly turn pork in pan to coat in the honey then set aside to rest for 5–10 minutes.

5. Place roast kumara in a bowl and use a fork or potato masher to very lightly crush the kumara. Fold through red onion, parsley and feta. Season to taste with salt and pepper.

6. Thinly slice pork, reserving any resting juices.

To serve, divide kumara feta crush and apple fennel salad between plates. Top with slices of pork and drizzle with any resting juices and remaining yoghurt dressing.

GF	DF (use coconut yoghurt and omit feta)		
		Energy	423kcal (1768kJ)
		Protein	35.0g
		Carbohydrate	38.4g (15.5g sugars)
		Fat	12.9g (4.20g sat fat)

LEMONGRASS BEEF VERMICELLI NOODLES WITH FRESH HERBS AND VEGETABLES.

Makes:	**4 portions**
Prep time:	**30 minutes**
Cook time:	**10 minutes**

500–550g lean beef rump,
 sirloin or eye fillet
1 onion, thinly sliced
3–4 spring onions, white and
 green part separated
 and each thinly sliced
3–4 tablespoons Lemongrass
 Paste (see page 257)
2 teaspoons oil

Dressing
⅓ cup freshly squeezed lime
 or lemon juice
2 tablespoons fish sauce
1 tablespoon water
1 tablespoon sweet chilli sauce
 (store-bought or see page 258)
½ red chilli, chopped (optional)
½ clove garlic, finely chopped

To serve
150g vermicelli or thin rice stick
 noodles
1 telegraph cucumber
3 carrots
1 cup each mint and coriander
 leaves
2 tablespoons chopped roasted
 cashew nuts or peanuts

Vietnamese cuisine uses loads of fresh herbs, fragrant ingredients such as lemongrass, and perfectly balanced dressings to achieve maximum flavour, whilst keeping dishes lean and healthy. This dish is the perfect example – light, fresh and full of flavour; don't skimp on the herbs, they're a key part!

Bring a medium pot of salted water to the boil.

1. Cut beef into 2–3cm chunks, and then very finely slice each chunk so you have very small, thin slices of beef. Combine with onion, white part of spring onion and lemongrass paste in bowl. Set aside to marinate for 15 minutes at room temperature while you prepare the rest of the meal (or marinate in the fridge overnight, if you have time).

2. Mix all dressing ingredients together in a bowl and set aside.

3. Cut cucumber into thirds, then cut each piece in half lengthways, scoop out seeds with a teaspoon, and slice into half moons; set aside on a plate. Peel and shred or coarsely grate carrots and set aside on plate with cucumber.

4. Cook noodles in pot of boiling water for a few minutes or until just cooked through (taste a noodle to determine). Drain, run under cold water to stop them sticking together then drain well again. Use scissors to snip noodles in a few places to shorten strands to make them easier to eat.

5. Meanwhile, heat half of the oil in a wok or your largest fry-pan on high heat. Add half of the marinated beef and stir-fry quickly for 2–3 minutes until just cooked through. Set aside in a bowl. Repeat with remaining oil and beef. Add green part of spring onions and continue cooking for 1–2 more minutes.

To serve, divide noodles, stir-fried beef, vegetables, herbs and nuts between serving bowls. Serve with bowl of dressing to spoon over and mix through noodles and vegetables just before eating.

Energy	447kcal (1870kJ)
Protein	33g
Carbohydrate	44.9g (11.7g sugars)
Fat	15.3g (4.5g sat fat)

LIME AND CHILLI-GLAZED FISH WITH
EDAMAME RADISH SALAD AND BROWN RICE.

143.

Makes:	4 portions
Prep time:	15 minutes
Cook time:	5 minutes

Lime and chilli-glazed fish

3 tablespoons sweet chilli sauce
  (store-bought or see page 258)
2–3 kaffir lime leaves, tough inner
  stalk removed and thinly sliced
2 tablespoons soy sauce
2 tablespoons lime juice
600g boneless, skinless white
  fish fillets

Edamame radish salad

4 baby radishes, thinly sliced
1 Lebanese cucumber, thinly sliced
2 cups frozen edamame beans,
  defrosted
8–10 mint leaves, thinly sliced
1 tablespoon pickled ginger,
  finely chopped

To serve

2 cups steamed brown rice

This is a super-quick and tasty meal. Use any fresh white fish. Feel free to sometimes mix it up by using salmon or chicken breast, which also work incredibly well with this tasty glaze and salad. We're willing to bet this could become one of your favourite fast mid-week meals!

Preheat oven to grill. Bring a half kettle of water to the boil. Line an oven tray with baking paper.

1. Mix sweet chilli sauce, kaffir lime leaf, soy sauce and lime juice together.

2. Place beans in a heatproof bowl or pot and cover with boiling water. Leave for a few minutes then drain.

3. Lay fish fillets on lined oven tray and spread with half of the glaze (reserve the rest). Season with a little salt and grill, on an upper oven rack, for 4–5 minutes or until fish is just cooked through and the glaze is caramelised.

4. In a bowl, toss together radishes, cucumber, beans, mint, pickled ginger and remaining glaze.

Divide salad between plates and top with a piece of glazed fish. Serve with steamed brown rice.

DF | GF (use GF soy sauce)

Energy 402kcal (1679kJ)
Protein 42.1g
Carbohydrate 44.6g (5.8g sugars)
Fat 5.1g (0.4g sat fat)

PARMESAN-CRUMBED CHICKEN
WITH BALSAMIC AND HONEY ROASTED VEG.

Makes:	4 portions
Prep time:	20 minutes
Cook time:	35 minutes

Balsamic and honey roasted veg

2 medium-large beetroot, scrubbed (leave skin on) and cut into 2cm cubes
1 red onion, diced 2cm
3 carrots, peeled and cut into batons
2 teaspoons olive oil
1 tablespoon balsamic vinegar
2 teaspoons honey
4 handfuls baby spinach
1 teaspoon extra-virgin olive oil
Juice of ½ lemon

Parmesan-crumbed chicken

⅓ cup finely grated Parmesan cheese
⅓ cup ground almonds or dried breadcrumbs
2–3 teaspoons finely chopped thyme or rosemary
550g skinless chicken breasts
1 teaspoon olive oil
1½–2 tablespoons tomato paste
Handful of fresh basil leaves

A healthier take on crumbed chicken, but with all the flavour and made gluten free by using ground almonds in the crumb. Roasting your root vegetables with a dash of balsamic and honey is an easy way to make them even more delicious by bringing out all their natural sweet flavours.

Preheat oven to 200°C. Line two oven trays with baking paper.

1. Toss beetroot, onion and carrots on one lined tray with olive oil, balsamic vinegar and honey. Spread out into a single layer, season with salt and pepper and roast for about 20 minutes until tender and slightly caramelised.

2. Mix Parmesan, ground almonds/breadcrumbs and rosemary/thyme in a small bowl.

3. Pat chicken dry with paper towels and cut horizontally into steaks; to do this, place your hand flat on top of a chicken breast and use a large sharp knife to carefully and evenly slice through horizontally to make two thin steaks. Rub with olive oil and season with salt and pepper. Spread ½–1 teaspoon of tomato paste over each steak and place on other lined tray.

4. After 20 minutes of roasting, remove vegetables from oven, give them a toss and return to oven for a further 10–15 minutes or until tender and golden. Sprinkle Parmesan crumb over chicken steaks and season with a little more salt and pepper. Bake chicken (on a rack above the vegetables) for 12 minutes or so, until cooked through and golden (you can switch the oven to grill for the last couple of minutes if you like).

5. Toss balsamic roasted vegetables with baby spinach, extra-virgin olive oil and lemon juice.

To serve, divide chicken and balsamic roasted vegetables between plates and garnish with basil.

GF (use ground almonds)

Energy	321kcal (1343kJ)
Protein	37.5g
Carbohydrate	17.3g (15.4g sugars)
Fat	10g (3.1g sat fat)

MISO AND LEMON-GLAZED CHICKEN WITH JAPANESE SESAME SPINACH AND AVOCADO SALAD.

147.

Makes:	4 portions
Prep time:	20 minutes
Cook time:	10 minutes

Japanese sesame dressing

1 tablespoon sesame seeds
2 tablespoons mayonnaise
2 teaspoons rice vinegar
1 tablespoon soy sauce
½ teaspoon honey
¼ teaspoon sesame oil

Salad

2 Lebanese cucumbers or
   1 telegraph cucumber
3–4 baby radishes
2 spring onions
Flesh of 1 firm ripe avocado
4–6 handfuls baby spinach
1 cup frozen edamame beans,
   defrosted

Miso and lemon-glazed chicken

1½ tablespoons white miso
   paste
1 teaspoon soy sauce
1 tablespoon rice vinegar
½ teaspoon honey
½ teaspoon sesame oil
1 teaspoon finely grated ginger
1½ tablespoons water
550g skinless chicken breasts
1 teaspoon oil
Juice of 1 lemon

Here's a healthy meal favourite using Japanese flavours of miso and sesame. This dish has got serious flavour – the miso glaze and creamy sesame dressing are as good as it gets! If you can't be bothered making the sesame dressing, you can buy Japanese goma (sesame) dressing from the international section at the supermarket.

1. To make the Japanese sesame dressing, toast sesame seeds in a dry fry-pan, moving the pan around frequently, for about 2 minutes or until light golden. Set aside about ½ teaspoon for garnish, then crush the rest of the sesame seeds in a mortar and pestle to form a paste. Combine sesame paste with remaining dressing ingredients and whisk until smooth (I just do this in the bowl of the mortar and pestle). Set dressing aside.

2. For the salad, cut cucumber in half lengthways, scoop out seeds with a teaspoon and thinly slice into half-moons; thinly slice baby radishes; thinly slice spring onions; slice avocado. Place in a large bowl with spinach and edamame.

3. Mix miso, soy sauce, rice vinegar, honey, sesame oil, ginger and water together in a small bowl.

4. Pat chicken dry with paper towels and cut into steaks; to do this, place one hand flat on top of a chicken breast and use a knife in the other hand to carefully slice through horizontally to make 2 thin steaks.

5. Heat oil in a large non-stick fry-pan on medium-high heat. Cook chicken steaks for 2–3 minutes each side or until cooked through. Set chicken aside and keep pan on the heat. Add miso mixture to the pan, bring to a rapid bubble and squeeze in lemon juice. Let it bubble for a minute, then turn off the heat. Return chicken steaks to the pan and toss to coat.

To serve, toss salad with dressing and divide between plates. Top with chicken steak (or slices of chicken), and spoon over any remaining glaze from pan. Garnish with a sprinkle of reserved toasted sesame seeds.

DF   GF (use GF miso and GF soy sauce)

Energy	428kcal (1791kJ)
Protein	38.5g
Carbohydrate	10.6g (5.1g sugars)
Fat	25g (4.5g sat fat)

PUMPKIN, CHICKPEA AND COURGETTE CURRY WITH BROWN RICE AND KACHUMBER.

Makes:	5 portions
Prep time:	20 minutes
Cook time:	20 minutes

1 teaspoon oil
1 red onion, diced
2 cloves garlic, finely chopped
2.5cm piece fresh ginger,
   peeled and cut into
   fine matchsticks
1½ teaspoons each ground
   cumin, ground coriander,
   garam masala
1 teaspoon ground turmeric
1 red or green chilli, seeds
   removed and thinly sliced
1 x 400g can chopped tomatoes
1 x 400g can lite coconut milk
700g peeled pumpkin, cut into
   3cm cubes
2 medium courgettes, sliced
2 x 400g cans chickpeas,
   rinsed and drained
3 handfuls baby spinach leaves

Kachumber
2–3 tomatoes, diced
¼ red onion, finely diced
1 Lebanese cucumber, seeds
   removed and finely diced
Juice of ½ lemon
½ cup chopped coriander and/
   or mint leaves

To serve
2 cups steamed brown or
   wild rice
¼ cup unsweetened natural
   yoghurt
2 tablespoons toasted flaked
   almonds or chopped roasted
   cashew nuts

A simple, healthy and yummy curry, which is perfect for portioning and freezing for those nights when you just want a quick tasty meal and can't be bothered cooking.

1. Heat oil in a large heavy-based pot on medium heat. Cook onion, garlic and ginger, with a good pinch of salt, for 2–3 minutes over a gentle heat until soft and fragrant.

2. Add spices and cook a further minute, then add chilli, tomatoes and coconut milk and bring to a simmer.

3. Add pumpkin and cook for 10–12 minutes or until tender. Season to taste with salt and pepper.

4. Add courgettes and chickpeas, and cook for a further 3–4 minutes. Taste again and season with more salt and pepper, if needed. Fold in the spinach until wilted and bright green.

5. Mix all kachumber ingredients together and season to taste with salt and pepper.

Serve with steamed brown or wild rice, a dollop of yoghurt on top of curry, a scatter of almonds/cashew nuts and the kachumber.

GF | V | DF (use coconut yoghurt)

Energy	449kcal (1878kJ)
Protein	15.4g
Carbohydrate	66.0g (17.3g sugars)
Fat	11.4g (6.2g sat fat)

Makes:	4 portions
Prep time:	10 minutes
Cook time:	15 minutes

Pea crush
2¾ cups frozen peas
1 cup chicken or vegetable
    stock
2 tablespoons finely chopped
    mint leaves
1 tomato, diced
1–2 teaspoons lemon juice
1 teaspoon butter or extra-
    virgin olive oil

Salmon and lemony greens
500g boneless, skinless
    salmon fillet, cut into
    4 even-sized portions
1 teaspoon olive oil
2 cloves garlic, chopped
Zest of ½ lemon
300g green beans, asparagus
    or broccolini (or a mixture
    of any/all), ends trimmed
Juice of 1 lemon
3 handfuls baby spinach
    or chopped spinach,
    silverbeet or kale (any
    tough stalks removed)
½ lemon, cut into wedges

We love salmon and all its goodness, especially with sweet peas and lemon. The pea crush is a beautiful match with simply seared salmon and lots of lemony greens.

1. Place peas and stock in a pot and bring to a simmer. Cook for 3–5 minutes until tender. Roughly crush or mash peas with a potato masher or fork – if there is still lots of leftover liquid, drain it. Mix in mint, tomato, lemon juice and butter/extra-virgin olive oil. Season to taste with salt and pepper and keep warm.

2. Pat salmon dry with paper towels and season with salt. Heat a large non-stick fry-pan on medium heat. Pan-fry salmon for about 2 minutes on each side until golden. Set aside to rest.

3. Return pan to the heat with olive oil. Sizzle garlic and lemon zest for 30 seconds, then add green beans/asparagus/broccolini and lemon juice to cook for a few minutes until just tender. Add leafy greens, toss together until just wilted and season with a pinch of salt.

To serve, spoon pea crush onto plates, top with a piece of salmon and lemony greens. Serve with lemon wedges to squeeze over.

GF   DF (use olive oil)

Energy	446kcal (1866kJ)
Protein	30.1g
Carbohydrate	9g (4g sugars)
Fat	31.2g (9.1g sat fat)

CHINESE STEAMED FISH PARCELS WITH STIR-FRIED MUSHROOMS, ASPARAGUS, GINGER AND CHILLI.

Makes:	4 portions
Prep time:	20 minutes
Cook time:	10 minutes

Sauce

3 tablespoons soy sauce

1½ teaspoons sesame oil

1½ cloves garlic, minced

1 red chilli, seeds removed and finely chopped (leave a few seeds in if you like some heat)

2 tablespoons chopped coriander stalks (reserve leaves for garnish)

2cm piece fresh ginger, peeled and cut into very fine matchsticks

600g boneless, skinless white fish fillets (e.g. snapper, tarakihi, gurnard, John dory, blue cod)

1 teaspoon oil

½ teaspoon sesame oil

100g fresh shiitake mushrooms, thinly sliced

1 bunch asparagus, ends trimmed and cut into thirds

4 baby bok choy, cut in half lengthways

1 teaspoon cornflour mixed with 2 tablespoons water

2 teaspoons rice vinegar

To serve

2 cups steamed brown or wild rice

¼ cup coriander leaves

We love steaming fresh fish in its own juices, and the result is especially delicious using the Chinese flavours of soy, sesame and coriander. Steaming keeps the fish moist and tender, just be careful not to overcook it. If asparagus is out of season, you could use broccolini or broccoli, and if you can't get fresh shiitake mushrooms, button mushrooms will do.

Preheat oven to 180°C.

1. Mix all sauce ingredients together and divide equally between two small bowls.

2. Lay 4 rectangles of tinfoil (about 40cm long) on the bench and place a fish fillet in the centre of each. Spoon one bowl of the sauce over fish fillets, dividing equally between parcels. Fold over tinfoil and wrap up to make parcels. Place on an oven tray and bake for 6–8 minutes (depending on thickness of fish fillets) or until fish is just cooked through.

3. Meanwhile, heat oil and sesame oil in a wok or your largest fry-pan on medium-high heat. Cook mushrooms for a few minutes, adding 1–2 tablespoons of water to help them cook, until soft. Add asparagus and bok choy, stir-fry for about 2 minutes, adding 1–2 tablespoons of water to help them cook. Add cornflour mixture, vinegar and the remaining bowl of sauce. Continue stir-frying for about 2 minutes until vegetables are just tender and sauce has thickened slightly.

To serve, divide rice and stir-fried vegetables between plates. Open steamed fish parcels and transfer to plates, along with any juices from the parcels. Garnish with coriander leaves.

DF	GF (use GF soy sauce)		
		Energy	360kcal (1504kJ)
		Protein	38.9g
		Carbohydrate	36.8g (4.9g sugars)
		Fat	6.2g (0.9g sat fat)

THAI GREEN CHICKEN CURRY
WITH LIME LEAF, PEAS, COURGETTE,
BEANS AND CAULIFLOWER 'RICE'.

Makes:	4 portions
Prep time:	15 minutes
Cook time:	15 minutes

1 teaspoon oil
1 onion, diced
2 tablespoons Thai Green Curry
    Paste (store-bought or see
    page 257)
1 x 400g can lite coconut milk
2 kaffir lime leaves, tough stem
    removed and thinly sliced
1 teaspoon sweet chilli sauce
    (store-bought or see page 258)
1–2 teaspoons fish sauce
500g boneless, skinless
    chicken thighs or breast, diced
2 medium courgettes, sliced
1½ cups frozen peas
150g green beans, trimmed
    and cut in half

To serve
Asian herbs (e.g. coriander,
    mint, Thai basil)
Cauliflower Rice (see page 243)
1 lime or ½ lemon, cut into
    wedges

Deliciously creamy and fragrant, a Thai green curry is always popular. Use a good quality store-bought curry paste to fast-track this recipe or have a go at making your own curry paste (with our recipe on page 257) which you can freeze. Feel free to use fish instead of chicken for a Thai Green Fish Curry.

1. Heat oil in a large fry-pan on medium heat. Add onion and cook for 4–5 minutes until soft. If at any time onion is sticking to the bottom of the pan and burning, add 1–2 tablespoons of water, stir, and it should unstick.

2. Add curry paste and 3–4 tablespoons of the coconut milk, stir together until smooth and cook for 2–3 minutes until the paste is fragrant.

3. Add remaining coconut milk, kaffir lime leaves, sweet chilli sauce and fish sauce, stir and simmer for 3–4 minutes. Add chicken to simmering sauce, cover and cook for about 5 minutes before adding courgette, peas and beans; continue to cook for a further 3–4 minutes or until chicken is just cooked through. Season to taste with more fish sauce if needed.

Scatter fresh herbs over the curry and serve with cauliflower rice. Squeeze over lime or lemon just before eating.

DF	GF

Energy	443kcal (1851kJ)
Protein	39.8g
Carbohydrate	20.3g (16.1g sugars)
Fat	20.8g (12.9g sat fat)

**THAI PORK SALAD
WITH TAMARIND GLAZE.**

Makes:	4 portions
Prep time:	20 minutes
Cook time:	10 minutes

Salad

1 mango (slightly under-ripe
    is best)
1 telegraph cucumber
200g snow peas
1–1½ red chillies (optional)
2 kaffir lime leaves
¼ cup chopped coriander
¼ cup torn mint leaves
2 cups mung bean sprouts
⅓ cup roasted peanuts,
    roughly chopped

Pork

550g lean pork fillet (at room
    temperature)
2 teaspoons Chinese five-spice
    powder
1 teaspoon oil
¼ cup tamarind juice (see tip)
1 tablespoon honey

Dressing

Juice of 1½ lemons
1½ tablespoons rice vinegar
1½ teaspoons fish sauce
1½ teaspoons honey

To serve

¼ cup roughly chopped
    roasted peanuts
Chopped coriander
1 lime, cut into quarters

A super fresh and lively salad with lean pork; however, use chicken breast or even tofu or lean lamb or beef if you prefer.

1. Start by prepping the salad. Peel mango and slice flesh; cut cucumber in half lengthways, scoop out seeds with a teaspoon, then thinly slice; remove tough stringy bit from snow peas and slice in half lengthways; cut chilli (if using) in half lengthways, remove seeds and thinly slice; remove tough stem from lime leaves and thinly slice. Place all in a large bowl, along with herbs, bean sprouts and peanuts.

2. Pat pork dry with paper towels, coat in five-spice powder and season well with salt. Heat oil in a medium or large fry-pan on medium-high heat. Cook pork for about 3 minutes on each side or until just cooked through. Meanwhile, mix tamarind juice and honey together in a small bowl.

3. Once pork is cooked, set aside to rest, keep pan on heat and pour in tamarind mixture – allow it to bubble for a minute or two until reduced and sticky. Slice pork, return to the pan and spoon over the glaze to coat.

4. Mix dressing ingredients together and, when ready to eat, toss with salad.

To serve, divide salad between plates and top with pork and tamarind glaze. Garnish with a few more peanuts, coriander and a lime wedge to squeeze over.

Tip: To make tamarind juice, mix tamarind paste or pulp with boiling water according to packet instructions. Tamarind can be found in the international section of many supermarkets but if you can't get hold of it, just use the juice of ½ lemon.

DF	GF

Energy	384kcal (1604kJ)
Protein	36.7g
Carbohydrate	31.5g (19.7g sugars)
Fat	11.8g (2.6g sat fat)

Makes:	4 portions
Prep time:	20 minutes
Cook time:	20 minutes

Super grain salad
⅓ cup bulghur wheat, freekah or brown rice
⅓ cup quinoa
1 cup water
1 red capsicum
½ telegraph cucumber
¼ red onion
1 carrot
¼ cup Asian Dressing (see page 256)

Lemongrass chicken
2 teaspoons oil
550g lean chicken mince
3–4 tablespoons Lemongrass Paste (see page 257)
¼ teaspoon salt
Pinch of chilli flakes, chilli powder or cayenne powder (optional)
¼ cup chopped coriander

To serve
1 baby romano or cos lettuce, leaves separated
100g mung bean sprouts
¼ cup chopped mint leaves
2 tablespoons chopped roasted peanuts
1 tablespoon hot chilli sauce, e.g. Sriracha (optional)
½ lemon or 1 lime, cut into wedges

One of our very first Fresh Start recipes, which was rated a hit by customers. Packing tasty stir-fried chicken mince and vegetables into lettuce cups is a fun way to eat this dish and you're guaranteed to feel healthy and satisfied afterwards. To make gluten free, replace the bulghur wheat with brown or wild rice.

1. Place bulghur/freekah/brown rice and quinoa, water and a pinch of salt in a small pot and bring to the boil. As soon as it boils, cover with a lid and reduce to low heat to cook for 15 minutes. Turn off heat and leave to steam, still covered, for a further 5 minutes before fluffing up with a fork.

2. Meanwhile, prep the rest of the salad ingredients. Remove core and seeds from capsicum and finely dice; cut cucumber in half lengthways, use a teaspoon to scoop out seeds and thinly slice; finely dice red onion; peel carrot and shred or coarsely grate. Place all in a bowl with Asian Dressing.

3. Heat oil in a large fry-pan on high heat. Cook chicken mince, lemongrass paste, salt and chilli/cayenne (if using) for about 5 minutes, or until cooked through and any liquid has evaporated. Use a wooden spoon to break up chicken mince as it cooks. Transfer to a bowl and stir through coriander.

4. Add cooked grains to salad and toss to combine. Taste, and season with salt and pepper, if needed.

To serve, divide lettuce leaves between plates. Fill each leaf with super grain salad and lemongrass chicken. Top with mung bean sprouts, mint, peanuts, and a little chilli sauce (if using). Squeeze over lemon/lime wedges just before eating.

Energy	348kcal (1453kJ)
Protein	37.8g
Carbohydrate	23.5g (7.5g sugars)
Fat	10.7g (2g sat fat)

CREAMY KUMARA AND LENTIL CURRY WITH CAULIFLOWER RICE AND KACHUMBER.

Makes:	4 portions
Prep time:	20 minutes
Cook time:	30 minutes

Kumara and lentil curry
1 teaspoon oil
1 brown onion, thinly sliced
3 tablespoons Lemongrass
    Paste (see page 257)
1 tablespoon yellow curry paste
1 x 400g can lite coconut milk
¾ cup split red lentils
200g red kumara, scrubbed
    (leave skin on) and diced 1cm
1½ cups water
1–1½ tablespoons soy sauce
1 teaspoon coconut sugar
    or honey
100–150g baby spinach leaves
    or finely sliced kale leaves
Juice of ½ lemon

Kachumber
2–3 tomatoes, diced
¼ red onion, finely diced
1 Lebanese cucumber, seeds
    removed, finely diced
Juice of ½ lemon
½ cup chopped coriander
    and/or mint leaves

To serve
Cauliflower Rice (see page 243)

Here's one of our customers' favourite vegetarian dishes from Fresh Start – a lovely kumara and lentil curry with lemongrass and coconut. It's served with cauliflower rice to include even more vegetables; however, you could serve it with steamed brown rice (½ cup per portion), if you prefer.

Preheat oven to 220°C.

1. Heat oil in a medium-sized pot on medium heat. Cook onion for 3–4 minutes, until softened. Add lemongrass paste, yellow curry paste and 2–3 tablespoons of the coconut milk, and cook, stirring, for 1–2 minutes until fragrant. If mixture starts to stick at all, add a little more coconut milk.

2. Add remaining coconut milk, lentils, kumara, water, soy sauce and coconut sugar/honey and bring to the boil. Lower heat and simmer for 15–20 minutes, stirring often, until lentils and kumara are tender. If the curry is looking dry, add ¼–½ cup water. Remove from heat and stir through spinach until wilted.

3. While curry is cooking, prepare the cauliflower 'rice'.

4. Mix all kachumber ingredients together and season with a little salt and pepper. Once curry is cooked, stir through lemon juice and season to taste with salt (if needed).

To serve, spoon cauliflower rice and curry onto plates, and serve with kachumber.

DF | V | GF (use GF soy sauce)

Energy	423kcal (1770kJ)
Protein	17.3g
Carbohydrate	47.6g (18.2g sugars)
Fat	15.5g (8.1g sat fat)

chapter
four—

comfort food

- *We don't believe in denying yourself* foods you love so this section has lots of favourites like burgers, pizza and mac 'n' cheese, but with a more nutritious, homemade twist! However, there's also nothing wrong with getting takeaways or eating out every now and again, as long as you eat them in balance and moderation.

- *If you do get takeaways, do it the smart (and delicious) way* – watch portion sizes and add in vegetables to help fill you up and make the meal more nutritious (AND cut the calories in half!). For example, if it's Fish 'n' Chips, portion out a small handful of chips and add a big side salad. If getting Indian, portion out ½ cup rice, skip the naan bread, and make a raita (yoghurt, mint, grated cucumber and tomato) to go with the meal. If it's a burger, get it in a lettuce 'bun', or just have one half of the bread bun.

- *If you're dining out, check out the menu online before* going to the restaurant so you know what options you have and you can plan ahead. *Snack on vegetable sticks before you go* out so you're not ravenous when you get there and want to order everything or snack on the bread! Order two entrées (as your entrée and main), or entrée and dessert and a side of vegetables.

- Having a few homemade pizza bases or meat patties in the freezer means that you can quickly whip up healthy Friday night pizza or burgers!

ALMOND-CRUMBED CHICKEN NUGGETS WITH KUMARA FRIES AND HERBY SLAW.

Makes:	**4 portions**
Prep time:	**20 minutes**
Cook time:	**20 minutes**

Nuggets
½ cup ground almonds
⅓ cup finely grated
    Parmesan cheese
1½ tablespoons finely
    chopped thyme
¾ teaspoon salt
1 carrot, peeled, or courgette
500g lean chicken mince
2–3 teaspoons olive oil

Kumara fries
300g red kumara, scrubbed
    (leave skin on)
1 teaspoon olive oil

To serve
Herby Slaw (see page 240)
¼ cup Tomato Sauce
    (see page 237)

Coating these nuggets in ground almonds and Parmesan gives them a tasty golden, crunchy coating that's also gluten free. A hit with both kids and adults, especially when served with our refined sugar-free Tomato Sauce (see page 237).

Preheat oven to 200°C. Line a large oven tray with baking paper.

1. In a medium shallow bowl or dish, mix ground almonds, Parmesan, thyme and salt.

2. Grate carrot or courgette straight onto a clean tea towel, then wring out as much excess moisture as you can. In a large bowl, mix carrot/courgette with chicken mince and ⅓ cup of the ground almond mixture (reserve the rest for coating). Season with salt and pepper.

3. Roll small golf ball-sized balls of chicken mixture, placing on a clean, dry plate as you go. Place in the fridge for 5–10 minutes to firm up a little.

4. While chicken balls chill, cut kumara into 1–2cm-wide fries and toss with olive oil on lined tray. Spread out in a single layer, season well with salt and pepper and roast for about 20 minutes until golden.

5. Coat each chicken ball in almond crumb mixture and flatten slightly into a nugget shape.

6. Heat half of the olive oil in a large non-stick fry-pan on medium heat. Brown nuggets in two batches (using remaining oil for second batch), for about 2 minutes on each side until golden, then transfer to oven tray with kumara chips to finish cooking through for 5 minutes.

Serve nuggets and fries with Herby Slaw and Tomato Sauce.

GF

Energy	445kcal (1860kJ)
Protein	39.5g
Carbohydrate	32g (12.4g sugars)
Fat	16.8g (3.5g sat fat)

Makes:	6 portions
Prep time:	30 minutes
Cook time:	50 minutes

Kumara layers and topping
2 medium kumara (about 600g, orange, red or golden), scrubbed (leave skin on)
1 teaspoon olive oil, for brushing

Beef, mushroom and eggplant sauce
1 teaspoon olive oil
450g lean beef mince
1 onion, diced
250g button mushrooms, finely diced
1 medium eggplant, finely diced
2 tablespoons chopped thyme
1 x 400g can crushed tomatoes
1 cup salt-reduced beef or chicken stock
2 tablespoons tomato paste
2 tablespoons Worcestershire sauce

Creamy cauliflower cheese sauce
1 teaspoon olive oil
½ onion, diced
1 clove garlic, finely chopped
½ medium head cauliflower, chopped into florets
½ cup milk
½ cup salt-reduced chicken or vegetable stock
½ teaspoon Dijon mustard
½ cup grated Parmesan cheese

To serve
Green Salad (see page 251)

Our take on this comfort food classic uses rounds of roasted kumara as the layers between a rich beef and mushroom sauce, topped off with a creamy cauliflower cheese sauce. The result? A much healthier, veggie-packed lasagne that's a winner with the whole family!

Preheat oven to 200°C. Line an oven tray with baking paper.

1. Slice kumara into 0.5cm-thick rounds and arrange on lined oven tray. Brush or spray with olive oil. Season with salt and pepper and roast for 15 minutes or until golden (they do not have to be tender all the way through). Set aside on the bench to cool.

2. For the beef sauce, heat olive oil in a large fry-pan on medium-high heat. Cook beef, with a good pinch of salt, until browned, breaking up with a wooden spoon as it cooks. Set cooked mince aside. Add onion, mushrooms, eggplant and a good pinch of salt to the pan; cook for 8–10 minutes until vegetables are soft. Stir in remaining sauce ingredients and the cooked beef mince, and simmer for 8–10 minutes until sauce is thick and most of the liquid has evaporated.

3. For the creamy cauliflower sauce, on a separate element heat olive oil in a medium pot over medium heat. Cook onion, with a pinch of salt, for 2–3 minutes until soft but not coloured. Add garlic and continue cooking for 1 more minute. Add cauliflower, milk and stock. Cover partially and simmer for about 15 minutes or until cauliflower is soft.

4. Stir in mustard and half the Parmesan, then use a blender or stick blender to purée cauliflower and its cooking liquid together until silky smooth. Season to taste with salt and pepper.

5. To assemble lasagne, spread ½ cup of the beef mince sauce out in the base of a medium-large baking/lasagne dish. Cover with a single layer of kumara rounds (about one-third of the kumara) then top evenly with half of the remaining beef sauce. Repeat with one more layer of kumara and beef sauce and a final layer of kumara. Finally, pour creamy cauliflower cheese sauce all over the top and sprinkle over remaining Parmesan. Bake for 25 minutes, switching to grill for the last few minutes, until golden on top.

Allow lasagne to rest for at least 10 minutes before cutting up. Serve with green salad.

GF   (use GF Worcestershire sauce)

Energy	385kcal (1610kJ)
Protein	28.1g
Carbohydrate	36.4g (13.9g sugars)
Fat	12.4g (4.4g sat fat)

GRILLED EGGPLANT OR MUSHROOM BEEF BURGERS WITH KASUNDI AND HERBY SLAW.

Makes:	4 portions
Prep time:	15 minutes
Cook time:	20 minutes

550g lean beef or lamb mince
(or a mixture of both)
½ onion, grated
¾ teaspoon salt
½ teaspoon each ground cumin
and ground coriander
1 large eggplant, cut into 8
rounds, or 8 large Portobello
mushrooms, stalks removed
or trimmed
2–3 teaspoons olive oil

Kasundi
½ teaspoon olive oil
¼ teaspoon each coriander
seeds, cumin seeds and
fennel seeds, crushed
½ x 400g can crushed or
chopped tomatoes
1 teaspoon honey or
maple syrup
¼ teaspoon chilli flakes
(optional)

To serve
4 fancy lettuce leaves
2 tomatoes, sliced
½ red onion, thinly sliced
4 pickled gherkins, sliced
¼ cup mint leaves or chopped
coriander
Herby Slaw (see page 240)

Skip the bread but keep all the flavour and up the veggies with these burgers served between slices of grilled eggplant or mushrooms. Kasundi is a spiced tomato chutney that makes a delicious, easy accompaniment to these burgers.

1. Place mince, onion, salt and spices in a mixing bowl and use your clean hands to mix everything together until well combined. Divide and shape into 4 patties, about 1.5cm thick.

2. Preheat BBQ grill plate, or a large grill pan or fry-pan on medium-high heat. Brush eggplant slices or mushrooms and burger patties with olive oil and season with salt. Grill for about 5 minutes on each side until browned and cooked through. Keep warm. Alternatively, you can bake eggplant slices/mushrooms in a 220°C preheated oven (on an oven tray lined with baking paper) for 15–20 minutes, turning after 10 minutes.

3. To make the kasundi, heat oil in a small or medium fry-pan on medium heat. Add spices and allow to sizzle for 30 seconds, being careful they don't burn. Tip in tomatoes, honey/maple syrup and chilli flakes (if using), bring to a simmer and cook, stirring often, for 4–5 minutes until thickened to a chutney consistency. Season to taste with salt and pepper.

To serve, stack a slice of grilled eggplant or a mushroom (gill-side up) on each plate and top with lettuce, a burger patty, tomato, red onion, gherkins and finish with a second slice of grilled eggplant/mushroom. Top with a spoonful of kasundi and garnish with mint or coriander. Serve with Herby Slaw on the side.

GF | DF (omit slaw)

Energy	363kcal (1519kJ)
Protein	38.7g
Carbohydrate	16.4g (14.8g sugars)
Fat	14.2g (4.9g sat fat)

CHICKEN AND BEAN CHILLI
WITH TORTILLA CHIPS AND AVOCADO SALSA.

175.

Makes:	5 portions
Prep time:	20 minutes
Cook time:	20 minutes

Tortilla chips
4 small wheat or corn tortillas
1 teaspoon oil, for brushing
½ teaspoon Mexican Seasoning
    (store-bought or see page 256)

Chicken and bean chilli
1 teaspoon oil
1 onion, finely diced
1 carrot, peeled and grated
2 tablespoons Mexican Seasoning
    (store-bought or see page 256)
2 cloves garlic, finely chopped
Pinch of chilli flakes/powder or
    cayenne powder (optional)
450g lean chicken mince
2–3 tablespoons tomato paste
1½ cups salt-reduced chicken
    stock
¼ cup water
1 x 400g can black beans,
    rinsed and drained
1 x 400g can chopped tomatoes
2–3 tablespoons chipotle sauce
1 teaspoon runny honey
½ teaspoon vinegar (e.g. red
    wine, white wine, cider)

Avocado salsa
3 tomatoes
½ small red onion
1 Lebanese or ½ telegraph
    cucumber
Flesh of 1 firm ripe avocado
¼ cup chopped coriander or
    parsley
Juice of ½ lemon or 1 lime

We love Mexican food, so here's our popular chicken and bean chilli recipe, served with crunchy homemade tortilla chips and a salsa made from lots of fresh avocado, cucumber, tomato and coriander. Feel free to change it up and serve with brown rice (½ cup per portion) instead of the tortilla chips. If you love your Mexican food spicy, make sure you up the chilli flakes and chipotle.

Preheat oven to 180°C.

1. For the tortilla chips, stack tortillas and cut into 8 triangles. Arrange in a single layer on a large oven tray and brush lightly with olive oil. Sprinkle with Mexican seasoning and a pinch of salt. Bake for 6–10 minutes or until golden and crisp (watch they don't burn). Set aside to cool.

2. To make chilli, heat oil in a large fry-pan on medium-high heat. Cook onion and carrot with a pinch of salt for 3–4 minutes, stirring regularly, until starting to soften. Add Mexican seasoning, garlic and chilli/cayenne (if using) and cook for a further 30 seconds, until fragrant.

3. Add chicken and a pinch of salt and cook for about 3 minutes, breaking mince up with a wooden spoon, until nearly cooked through. Stir through remaining ingredients and bring to a simmer. Reduce heat and simmer for 10–15 minutes, stirring occasionally, until sauce has thickened slightly. If looking dry, add ¼ cup more water. Season to taste with salt and pepper.

4. While chilli is cooking, prep vegetables for the avocado salsa. Dice tomatoes; finely dice red onion; cut cucumber in half lengthways, scoop out seeds with a teaspoon and dice; dice avocado. Add all to a bowl, toss with coriander/parsley and lemon juice and season to taste with salt and pepper.

To serve, divide chicken and bean chilli between bowls and top with salsa. Serve with tortilla chips on the side.

Energy	440kcal (1841kJ)
Protein	30.2g
Carbohydrate	41.7g (11g sugars)
Fat	16.1g (2.3g sat fat)

**CHICKEN, MANGO AND FETA PIZZA
WITH A WHOLEMEAL YOGHURT BASE.**

Makes:	4 portions (2 pizzas, ½ pizza per portion)
Prep time:	30 minutes
Cook time:	15 minutes

Wholemeal yoghurt pizza base
1½ cups wholemeal flour (185g), plus extra for kneading
2 teaspoons baking powder
¼ teaspoon ground turmeric
¼ teaspoon fennel seeds
½ teaspoon salt
1 cup unsweetened natural Greek yoghurt

Topping
3 tablespoons mango or other fruit chutney
2 tablespoons tomato paste
250g cooked chicken breast or thigh (about 1 large breast or 3 thighs), shredded
½ red onion, thinly sliced
1 punnet (250g) cherry tomatoes, cut in half
50g soft feta, crumbled
½ cup grated mozzarella

Ribbon salad
2 Lebanese or ½ a telegraph cucumber
2 carrots
Juice of 1 lemon
2 tablespoons chopped mint

To serve
½ cup natural unsweetened Greek yoghurt
½–1 teaspoon curry powder
Chopped coriander

Some would say that mixing Italian and Indian flavours might be a bit of a faux pas, but we reckon it works awesomely! This pizza has hints of sweet and spicy Indian flavours, and we love the fact that the base is made with yoghurt and wholemeal flour (and is so quick and easy to make!).

Preheat oven to 220°C. Preheat 2 pizza stones or oven trays in the oven.

1. Mix wholemeal flour, baking powder, turmeric, fennel seeds and salt in a large bowl. Make a well in the centre and add yoghurt, mix together and then transfer to a clean, lightly floured surface. Knead the dough for 4–5 minutes, adding a little extra flour as needed until the dough is smooth and pliable.

2. Cut dough into two pieces and leave to rest for at least 10 minutes while you prep the toppings. On a piece of baking paper, roll each piece of dough out to roughly 0.25–0.5cm thickness and 25cm diameter (rolling it out on baking paper will make it much easier to transfer the pizza to the oven later!).

3. Mix mango chutney and tomato paste, and spread over each pizza base. Scatter with chicken, red onion, cherry tomatoes, feta and mozzarella. Transfer pizzas (by lifting with baking paper) to hot pizza stones or oven trays. Bake for 14–15 minutes, swapping the positioning of the pizzas halfway through (so they get a chance to cook evenly), or until golden.

4. While the pizzas cook, prep the ribbon salad. Peel cucumber (stopping when you get to the watery core) and carrots into ribbons with a vegetable peeler; place in a bowl and toss with lemon juice, mint and a pinch of salt.

5. Mix yoghurt and curry powder together and season to taste with salt and pepper.

To serve, pile a small handful of salad ribbons on top of each pizza, dollop with yoghurt sauce and scatter with coriander. Cut each pizza into 6 even slices and serve with the remaining ribbon salad on the side.

Energy	447kcal (1868kJ)
Protein	31.9g
Carbohydrate	42.5g (9.8g sugars)
Fat	14.9g (8.9g sat fat)

Makes:	4 portions
Prep time:	20 minutes
Cook time:	25 minutes

Kumara Parmesan topping

400g orange kumara, peeled and diced

½ head cauliflower, stalk and florets roughly diced

¼ cup grated Parmesan cheese

Creamy chicken and thyme filling

2 teaspoons olive oil

550g boneless, skinless chicken thighs

1 leek, white and pale green part only, cut in half lengthways and thinly sliced

2 stalks celery, finely diced

2 cloves garlic, finely chopped

1 tablespoon chopped thyme

2–3 tablespoons water

1 cup salt-reduced chicken stock

2 teaspoons soy sauce

125g pottle lite sour cream

1 tablespoon cornflour, mixed with 1 tablespoon cold water

2–3 teaspoons wholegrain mustard

To serve

2–3 tablespoons chopped parsley

Sautéed Veggies (see page 248) or Green Salad (see page 251)

It's hard to beat a hearty, warming chicken pie, especially come autumn and winter. Have your pie and eat it too, with our delicious version that will please both your taste buds and waistline.

Preheat oven grill to high. Bring a medium pot of salted water to the boil. Set aside a medium casserole or pie dish (about 20 x 22cm or similar).

1. Cook kumara and cauliflower in boiling water for about 15 minutes, until tender. Drain well and tip back into pot. Roughly mash and season to taste with salt and pepper.

2. While veggies cook, prepare filling. Heat 1 teaspoon of the oil in a large fry-pan on high heat. Pat chicken dry, season with salt and pepper, and cook for about 3 minutes each side until golden (it does not need to be cooked all the way through), remove from pan and set aside. Keep pan on medium-high heat.

3. Add remaining oil to pan and cook leek, celery, garlic, thyme and water for 4–5 minutes, until soft. Scrape bottom of pan with a wooden spoon to release any pan brownings. Roughly dice chicken into 1–2cm pieces. Return diced chicken with any resting juices to pan, along with stock and soy sauce. Bring to a simmer and cook for about 3 minutes, until chicken is cooked through.

4. Reduce heat to low, stir through sour cream, cornflour mixture and mustard, and cook for about 1 minute, until the filling has slightly thickened. Remove from heat and season to taste with salt and pepper.

5. Transfer filling to casserole or pie dish. Top with dollops of mash and roughly spread out with a fork. Sprinkle with Parmesan and grill (on upper oven rack) for 4–5 minutes. Leave to rest in dish for 5 minutes before garnishing with parsley.

To serve, portion pie onto plates and serve with sautéed veggies or green salad.

GF (use GF soy sauce)

Energy	428kcal (1789kJ)
Protein	36.4g
Carbohydrate	29.4g (16.1g sugars)
Fat	17.3g (6.3g sat fat)

CREAMY MUSHROOM STEAK WITH ROOT VEG CHIPS.

Makes:	**4 portions**
Prep time:	**20 minutes**
Cook time:	**20 minutes**

Creamy mushrooms
1 punnet (250g) button
    mushrooms
1 teaspoon olive oil
1 onion, thinly sliced
¾ cup salt-reduced beef or
    chicken stock
1–2 teaspoons soy sauce
125g pottle lite sour cream
½ bag (75g) baby spinach
    leaves, chopped

Steak
550g lean beef sirloin or
    eye fillet steaks (at room
    temperature)
1 teaspoon olive oil

To serve
Root Veg Chips (see page 244)
2–3 tablespoons chopped
    parsley

A lovely piece of steak deserves a good creamy mushroom sauce, and this one does the job, along with packing in some extra vegetables. Served with some scrumptious caramelised root vegetable fries, it's a simple yet tasty meal.

Preheat oven to 220°C.

1. Start by making the root veg chips.
2. Use a pastry brush or paper towels to brush excess dirt off mushrooms (do not wash as they will absorb too much water), then slice and set aside.
3. Heat a large fry-pan on high heat. While pan heats, pat steaks dry with paper towels, rub with oil and season with salt and pepper. Cook for 2–3 minutes each side, for medium (depending on thickness), or until cooked to your liking. Set aside to rest, covered with foil, for 5 minutes.
4. While the steaks rest make the creamy mushrooms. Wash pan and return to medium heat with olive oil. Cook onion for a few minutes, stirring frequently, until softened and starting to brown. Add mushrooms and cook, stirring occasionally, for a further 3–4 minutes. Add stock and soy sauce to pan and simmer on low heat for 3–4 minutes.
5. In a small bowl, whisk sour cream with a few tablespoons of sauce from the pan until smooth, then stir back into pan.
6. Slice steak, reserving any resting juices. Stir spinach and any steak resting juices through mushroom sauce, season to taste with salt and pepper and remove from heat.

To serve, divide root veg chips and steak between plates, top with creamy mushroom sauce and scatter with parsley.

GF (use GF soy sauce)

Energy	444kcal (1855kJ)
Protein	38.6g
Carbohydrate	25.9g (21.3g sugars)
Fat	19.1g (7.4g sat fat)

HAWAIIAN GRILLED CHICKEN AND PINEAPPLE WITH AVOCADO IN A LETTUCE 'BUN'.

183.

Makes:	4 portions
Prep time:	20 minutes
Cook time:	10 minutes

1 tablespoon honey
2 teaspoons soy sauce
1 teaspoon tomato sauce
(store-bought or see
page 237)
1 teaspoon Worcestershire
sauce
Good pinch of chilli flakes
(optional)
550g skinless chicken breasts
1 teaspoon oil
4 slices fresh ripe pineapple
(cored), or 8 rings canned
pineapple (drained)

To serve
1 large iceberg lettuce
3–4 vine-ripened tomatoes,
sliced
Flesh of 1 firm ripe avocado,
sliced
½ red onion, very thinly sliced
8 teaspoons tomato chutney

When the sun is shining, fire up the barbie and grill the chicken and pineapple. If you have the time, marinate the chicken overnight.

1. In a medium dish, mix honey, soy, tomato and Worcestershire sauces and chilli flakes (if using). Pat chicken breasts dry with paper towels and cut horizontally into steaks – to do this, lay one hand flat on top of a chicken breast lying flat on a chopping board, then use a large sharp knife in the other hand to carefully slice through breast horizontally, trying to keep equal thickness on both sides. Toss chicken steaks in marinade to coat and set aside to marinate at room temperature for 10–15 minutes, or overnight in the fridge if you have time.

2. Heat oil in a large fry-pan on medium-high heat or preheat BBQ. Season chicken steaks with salt and pepper. Cook for 2–3 minutes on each side until golden and just cooked through. Set aside. Add pineapple rings to pan and cook for about 2 minutes each side until juicy and caramelised. Alternatively, do all the cooking on the BBQ grill or hotplate!

3. Wash and separate iceberg leaves and set 8 large leaves aside. Stack 2 leaves at a time and, if you like, use scissors to trim a nice, neat edge.

4. To serve, fill each 2-stack of iceberg leaves with grilled chicken and pineapple, tomato, avocado, red onion and 2 teaspoons tomato chutney. To eat, fold each iceberg stack over in half to enclose filling and make it easier to eat like a burger.

DF   GF (use GF soy sauce and Worcestershire sauce)

Energy	383kcal (1600kJ)
Protein	34.0g
Carbohydrate	22.6g (22.0g sugars)
Fat	16.3g (2.8g sat fat)

LENTIL AND CASHEW BURGERS WITH CARAMELISED ONIONS, AVO SMASH AND CREAMY CHIPOTLE.

Makes:	4 portions
Prep time:	25 minutes
Cook time:	20 minutes

Caramelised onions

1 teaspoon olive oil
2 brown onions, thinly sliced
1½ tablespoons balsamic vinegar
2 teaspoons honey

Lentil and cashew burgers

½ cup roasted cashew nuts
1 x 400g can brown lentils, rinsed
    and drained well
1 tablespoon tahini
½ red onion, grated or finely diced
1 free-range egg
Zest of ½ lemon
1 teaspoon soy sauce
1 teaspoon each sumac and
    lemon pepper
¼ cup finely chopped parsley
½ cup dried breadcrumbs
    or ground almonds
1 tablespoon GF or plain flour
2 teaspoons olive oil

Avo smash

Flesh of 1 firm ripe avocado
2 teaspoons lemon juice

Creamy chipotle

¼ cup unsweetened natural Greek
    yoghurt or coconut yoghurt or
    lite sour cream
1–2 tablespoons chipotle sauce

To serve

2 tomatoes, thinly sliced
½ telegraph cucumber, thinly sliced
1 baby cos lettuce or ½ iceberg
    lettuce, chopped
Pickled gherkins and jalapeños

These vegetarian burgers get the big tick – they're packed with flavour, protein and fibre, and both carnivores and vegetarians love them.

1. To make the caramelised onions, heat oil in a medium pot on medium heat. Cook onion for 7–8 minutes, stirring often, until starting to caramelise. If at any time the onion is sticking to the bottom of the pan and burning, add 1–2 tablespoons water, stir and it should unstick. Stir through balsamic vinegar and honey, cook a further 1–2 minutes then remove from heat and season to taste with salt and pepper.

2. While onions cook, make the lentil and cashew burgers. Crush cashews with a rolling pin (or in a food processor) and add to a medium bowl with half the lentils, tahini, onion, egg, lemon zest, soy sauce, spices and parsley. Mash well with a potato masher, until mixture has the consistency of hummus. Season with salt and pepper and stir through remaining lentils, breadcrumbs/ground almonds and flour.

3. Divide burger mixture into four and shape into patties, about 1cm thick. Set aside on a plate and dust each with a little flour.

4. Heat half of the oil in a large non-stick fry-pan on low-medium heat. Cook lentil burgers, two at a time, for 2–3 minutes each side, until golden brown and cooked through. You may need to add ½ teaspoon more oil when you flip the burgers, to help the crust crisp up. Set burgers aside to drain on a plate lined with paper towels.

5. In a small bowl, roughly mash avocado with lemon juice and season to taste with salt and pepper. In another small bowl, mix yoghurt/sour cream and chipotle sauce.

To serve, top each lentil and cashew burger with tomato, cucumber, avo smash, caramelised onions and place on a bed of lettuce. Drizzle with creamy chipotle and sprinkle with pickled gherkins and jalapeños.

Tip: If you have a food processor, save time by blitzing lentil burger ingredients until combined, then stir in remaining lentils, breadcrumbs/almonds and flour.

V
DF (use coconut yoghurt)
GF (use GF soy sauce, GF flour and ground almonds)

Energy	444kcal (1856kJ)
Protein	14.6g
Carbohydrate	30.8g (13.1g sugars)
Fat	27.7g (4.2g sat fat)

MAC 'N' CHEESE WITH BUTTERNUT, BACON, SAGE, SPINACH AND CREAMY CAULIFLOWER CHEESE SAUCE.

187.

Makes:	4 portions
Prep time:	30 minutes
Cook time:	35 minutes

Roast butternut

600g butternut or pumpkin,
   peeled and diced 1–2cm
2 slices lean bacon (e.g.
   shoulder or mid-eye),
   rind removed and diced
½ onion, diced
10–15 sage leaves, thinly sliced
1 tablespoon chopped thyme
1 teaspoon olive oil

Creamy cauliflower cheese sauce

1 teaspoon olive oil
½ onion, diced
1 clove garlic, finely chopped
½ medium head cauliflower,
   chopped into florets
⅔ cup milk
½ cup salt-reduced chicken
   or vegetable stock
¼ cup finely grated
   Parmesan cheese
1 tablespoon finely
   chopped parsley

Parmesan and parsley topping

¼ cup finely grated
   Parmesan cheese
1 tablespoon finely
   chopped parsley

220g dried macaroni (quinoa,
   wholemeal or standard)
2–2½ cups chopped spinach
   or silverbeet leaves

We couldn't have a comfort food section and not include this favourite! Our mac 'n' cheese is packed with vegetables and topped with a delicious creamy cauliflower cheese sauce.

Preheat oven to 220°C. Line an oven tray with baking paper.

1. Toss butternut, bacon and onion with sage, thyme and olive oil on lined tray. Spread out in a single layer, season with salt and pepper and roast for about 20 minutes, tossing once during cooking, until butternut is soft and slightly caramelised.

2. For the sauce, heat olive oil in a medium saucepan over medium heat. Cook onion and garlic, with a pinch of salt, for about 2 minutes until soft, but not coloured. Add cauliflower, milk and stock. Cover partially and simmer for about 15 minutes or until cauliflower is soft.

3. Meanwhile, in a separate pot, cook macaroni in boiling salted water until al dente (just cooked).

4. Stir Parmesan into cauliflower mixture, then use a blender or stick blender to purée cauliflower and its cooking liquid together until silky smooth. Add a little more milk if you think the sauce needs thinning out. Stir in parsley and season to taste with salt and pepper.

5. Switch oven to grill. Drain pasta, tip back into the pot and stir through spinach/silverbeet until wilted. Gently stir in roast butternut mixture. Spoon into 4 individual ramekins or one large baking dish. Spoon over cauliflower cheese sauce.

6. Mix Parmesan and parsley and sprinkle over the top, then grill for 5–10 minutes until golden.

GF (use quinoa macaroni)   V (omit bacon)

Energy	440kcal (1838kJ)
Protein	21.0g
Carbohydrate	61.8g (14.4g sugars)
Fat	10.5g (2.9g sat fat)

PUMPKIN, ROSEMARY, CHILLI AND MOZZARELLA PIZZA WITH A CAULIFLOWER CRUST BASE.

Makes:	2 portions (1 pizza, ½ pizza per portion)
Prep time:	15 minutes
Cook time:	55 minutes

Cauliflower crust base
400g (about 2½ cups) chopped cauliflower
1 small egg, lightly beaten
½ cup finely grated Parmesan cheese
1 clove garlic, finely chopped
½ teaspoon dried oregano or mixed herbs or cumin seeds or caraway seeds

Topping
¼ cup Pizza Sauce (see page 256)
¾ cup grated mozzarella
6 button mushrooms, sliced
200g peeled pumpkin, peeled into ribbons (with a vegetable peeler) or very thinly sliced
1 teaspoon olive oil
1 red chilli, finely chopped (remove seeds if you don't want too much heat)
1 tablespoon chopped rosemary leaves

To serve
Green Salad (see page 251)

Yes, you can make a lovely, golden crispy pizza base out of cauliflower! So you're eating vegetables without even knowing it. We love this topping combination of pumpkin, mushrooms, rosemary and chilli; however, feel free to mix and match this pizza base with our other favourite pizza topping combinations.

Preheat oven to 200°C and line an oven tray with baking paper.

1. Blitz cauliflower in a food processor until it has a fine, crumbly texture, like rice. Alternatively, you can grate the cauliflower.

2. Place crumbly cauliflower in a large bowl and microwave, uncovered, for about 6 minutes, or place on lined oven tray and bake for about 15 minutes, until just tender. Remove and transfer to a clean tea towel. When cool enough to handle, wring tea towel tightly to squeeze out as much water as you can.

3. Tip cauliflower into a large bowl, mix in egg, Parmesan, garlic and dried herbs/spices and season well with salt and pepper. Spoon mixture into the centre of the lined tray and spread out and flatten to make a circular or rustic pizza shape approximately 0.5cm thick. Bake for 30–40 minutes or until firm and golden around the edges.

4. Increase oven temperature to 220°C. Spread pizza sauce over the baked pizza crust and scatter over half of the mozzarella. Top with mushrooms and pumpkin ribbons, drizzle with olive oil, scatter with chilli and rosemary, then sprinkle with remaining mozzarella. Return to the oven to bake for 6–10 minutes or until the pumpkin is coloured and cheese bubbling.

To serve, cut pizza into 6 even slices. Serve with green salad.

GF	V

Energy	398kcal (1665kJ)
Protein	31.7g
Carbohydrate	17.6g (13.8g sugars)
Fat	20.9g (10g sat fat)

Makes:	4 portions
Prep time:	20 minutes
Cook time:	30 minutes

1 tablespoon butter or olive oil
1 large onion, finely diced
1 clove garlic, finely chopped
½ fennel bulb or stalk celery,
　　finely diced
1 carrot, peeled and finely diced
2 teaspoons curry powder
¼ cup white wine, chicken
　　stock or fish stock
2 tablespoons GF or plain flour
2 cups milk, heated to near boiling
1½ cups corn kernels (fresh,
　　canned and drained,
　　or frozen and defrosted)
2 handfuls chopped spinach
　　or silverbeet
400g good-quality smoked fish
　　(e.g. kahawai, snapper), flaked
1–2 boiled free-range eggs,
　　peeled and sliced (optional)
2 sheets filo pastry, cut in half
2 teaspoons melted butter or
　　olive oil, for brushing
2 tablespoons finely grated
　　Parmesan cheese

To serve
Green Salad (see page 251)
　　or Sautéed Veggies
　　(see page 248)

The smoked fish pie in the last Fresh Start book was a hit so here's another take, this time with a crispy filo pastry topping instead of mash. For a variation, you could substitute half of the smoked fish with chopped smoked mussels.

Preheat oven to 180°C.

1. Heat butter/olive oil in a large pot on medium heat. Cook onion, garlic, fennel/celery and carrot for 5–6 minutes on gentle heat until softened and fragrant but not coloured. Add curry powder and continue cooking for 1 more minute.

2. Add wine/stock and simmer 2–3 minutes until mostly evaporated. Sprinkle in flour, mix well to combine and coat the vegetables and cook for a few minutes. Gradually add the hot milk, ½ cup at a time, whilst stirring constantly to create a smooth sauce. Simmer for 2 minutes until thickened.

3. Stir in corn, spinach/silverbeet and three-quarters of the smoked fish and season to taste with salt and pepper. Half fill either one large baking dish or 4 individual ramekins with filling, top with boiled egg slices (if using) then top up with remaining filling and smoked fish.

4. Lightly brush or spray both sides of each piece of filo with melted butter/oil. Roughly scrunch the filo onto the top of each pie, tucking it in around the sides. Sprinkle with Parmesan. Place pie(s) on an oven tray to catch any drips and bake for 15 minutes until golden and crispy.

Serve with green salad or sautéed veggies.

Energy	447kcal (1869kJ)
Protein	41.9g
Carbohydrate	30.3g (11.4g sugars)
Fat	15.0g (4.3g sat fat)

SMOKED SALMON, DILL AND LEMON SOUR CREAM PIZZA WITH A QUINOA BASE.

Makes:	4 portions (2 pizzas, ½ pizza per portion)
Prep time:	15 minutes + 30 minutes rising time
Cook time:	15 minutes

Quinoa pizza base

½ cup warm water
½ teaspoon honey
1½ teaspoons active dried yeast
2 teaspoons olive oil
½ teaspoon salt
175g quinoa flour or GF flour
½ cup cooked quinoa

Topping

½ cup Pizza Sauce (see page 256)
½ red onion, thinly sliced
½ punnet cherry tomatoes, cut in half
1 cup grated mozzarella cheese
¼ cup lite sour cream or unsweetened natural Greek yoghurt
Finely grated zest and juice of ½ lemon
2 tablespoons chopped dill
2 teaspoons chopped capers
200g hot smoked salmon, flaked
2 handfuls rocket or baby spinach leaves

To serve

Green Salad (see page 251)

This pizza base recipe is gluten free, using quinoa and quinoa flour, but feel free to use GF flour or plain high-grade flour if you wish. Hot smoked salmon is intensely flavoured, so a little goes a long way. It's simply delicious on a pizza with a creamy caper, lemon and dill sauce drizzled over the top.

Preheat oven to 220°C. Preheat 2 pizza stones or oven trays in the oven.

1. Mix warm water and honey in a bowl, sprinkle over yeast and stir gently. Stand in a warm place for about 10 minutes until frothy. Mix in olive oil and salt.

2. Place flour and cooked quinoa in a mixing bowl and add yeast mixture. Mix well to form a dough (there may be some leftover flour in the bowl after you've formed the dough, which is fine, or the dough might feel a little too sticky, in which case add a tiny bit more flour).

3. Knead dough for a few minutes then place in a bowl, cover with a tea towel and leave in a warm place for about 30 minutes until doubled in size.

4. Once dough has risen, tip out onto a lightly floured bench and divide into two pieces. Roll each piece out on a large piece of baking paper into a disc about 0.5cm thick and 20–25cm in diameter (rolling it out on baking paper will make it much easier to transfer the pizza to the oven later!)

5. Spread each base with pizza sauce and scatter with onion, tomatoes and mozzarella. Transfer pizzas (by lifting with baking paper) to hot pizza stone or oven trays. Bake for 14–15 minutes, swapping the positioning of the pizzas halfway through (so they get a chance to cook evenly), or until golden.

6. Mix sour cream/yoghurt, lemon zest and juice, dill and capers in a small bowl.

7. Top cooked pizzas with flakes of smoked salmon and a handful of leafy greens. Drizzle with dill and lemon sour cream.

To serve, cut each pizza into 6 even slices. Serve with green salad.

GF

Energy	429kcal (1794kJ)
Protein	29.0g
Carbohydrate	40g (7.2g sugars)
Fat	16.7g (5.2g sat fat)

chapter
five—

smoothies, snacks, sides & extras

- Sometimes you'll need a snack to get you from one meal to the next, or if you're doing more exercise. This section has some great snack recipes, and here are some other quick and nutritious ideas:
  - ⅓ cup natural unsweetened yoghurt with a pinch of cinnamon and a small handful of berries
  - ½ apple or pear, sliced and spread with 1 tablespoon nut butter
  - chia seed pudding (1½ tablespoons chia seeds whisked with ½ cup milk and 1 teaspoon maple syrup. Chill in the fridge for a few hours or overnight until thickened and pudding-like)
  - Cucumber rounds with cottage cheese and a little smoked salmon
  - A piece of fruit
  - A small handful of cherry tomatoes
  - A hard-boiled egg
  - A handful of warmed-up edamame beans
  - A cup of warmed milk with cocoa, cinnamon and vanilla

- Smoothies make an awesome after-work or post-exercise snack – pre-chop and freeze smoothie ingredients such as banana, cauliflower, avocado, etc. and keep in zip-lock bags for instant, nutritious smoothies.

- As with all your meals, even if it's just a snack, serve your portion out on a little plate (e.g. a bliss ball or cookie) and put the rest away, out of sight, to avoid continuous picking or mindlessly grabbing for a second helping!

Makes:	16 portions
Prep time:	10 minutes + 2 hours chill time in the fridge

6 pitted medjool dates
¼ cup boiling water
½ cup raw or lightly toasted whole almonds
½ cup raw or lightly toasted hazelnuts
¾ cup desiccated coconut
½ cup rolled oats or quinoa flakes
2½ tablespoons coconut oil
2 tablespoons cacao or dark cocoa powder
¾ cup dried cherries or cranberries
Good pinch of salt
60g dark (e.g. 70% cocoa) chocolate, chopped
1 teaspoon coconut oil
Pinch of salt

1. Soak dates in boiling water for 5 minutes until soft.
2. Place almonds and hazelnuts in a food processor and whizz until fine crumbs. Add coconut, oats, coconut oil, cacao/cocoa, dates and soaking liquid, and most of the cherries/cranberries (reserve 1–1½ tablespoons for the top), and the salt, then pulse until well blended and sticky.
3. Press into a square baking tin or dish (about 20 x20 cm) lined with baking paper, and smooth down firmly with the back of a wet spoon.
4. Gently melt chocolate and second measure of coconut oil together in microwave or double boiler. Drizzle or spread over the mixture in the tin and dot with remaining chopped cherries or cranberries. Chill in the fridge for at least 2 hours before cutting into 16 squares/portions.

Store in an airtight container in the fridge for up to 2 weeks or freeze in zip-lock bags for up to 2 months.

V   DF   (use DF chocolate)   GF   (use quinoa flakes)

Energy	175kcal (733kJ)
Protein	3.3g
Carbohydrate	13.1g (11.9g sugars)
Fat	11.8g (5.9g sat fat)

SMOOTHIES.

Smoothies are awesome in so many ways – quick and easy to make, delicious to drink, and they help to bump up your fruit and veggie intake for the day. If you're not much of a breakfast person they can be a great way to ease into the day, or the perfect afternoon pick-me-up to keep you going until dinner. Making smoothies is so quick and convenient if you have some of your base ingredients (such as banana, butternut and cauliflower) pre-chopped and prepared and frozen in resealable bags – then all you have to do is grab them out of the freezer and get blending! Using frozen ingredients also gives an extra cold, thick and creamy result. Here are some of our favourite smoothie combinations.

Makes:	2 portions
Prep time:	5 minutes

1. Place all ingredients in a blender and blend until smooth. Pour into glasses and serve.

NUTTY SALTED CARAMEL.

2 pitted medjool dates
1½ bananas, peeled and chopped (ideally frozen)
⅔ cup cooled steamed cauliflower florets (ideally frozen)
1½ tablespoons smooth nut butter (e.g. peanut, cashew, almond)
Pinch of salt
¼ teaspoon vanilla extract
1⅔ cups almond milk
Handful of ice cubes

DF	V	GF

Energy	281kcal (1174kJ)
Protein	6.6g
Carbohydrate	43.4g (40.4g sugars)
Fat	12.2g (1.5g sat fat)

CREAMY CAULI, BERRY AND BANANA.

1 cup frozen mixed berries
1 banana, peeled and chopped (ideally frozen)
¾ cup cooled steamed cauliflower florets (ideally frozen)
2 tablespoons almond butter
¼ cup coconut yoghurt or coconut milk
½ teaspoon vanilla extract
1½ cups cold water
Handful of ice cubes

DF	V	GF

Energy	280kcal (1171kJ)
Protein	6.4g
Carbohydrate	24.4g (20.2g sugars)
Fat	17.2g (4.1g sat fat)

COOLING CUCUMBER, PINEAPPLE AND LIME.

1 cup chopped cucumber (ideally frozen)
1 banana, peeled and chopped (ideally frozen)
1½ cups peeled and chopped ripe pineapple
Juice of 1 lime or ½ lemon
Flesh of ½ medium avocado
½ cup coconut yoghurt or coconut milk
1⅓ cups cold water
Handful of ice cubes

DF	GF	V		Energy	390kcal (1631kJ)
				Protein	4.3g
				Carbohydrate	34g (31.1g sugars)
				Fat	25.6g (7.3g sat fat)

PLUM, BLACKCURRANT, BEETROOT AND SPICE.

½ cup frozen blackcurrants
½ cup peeled and chopped raw beetroot
¾ cup chopped dark-fleshed plums
    (e.g. black doris, Omega) (ideally frozen)
1 teaspoon maple syrup or honey
¼ teaspoon ground cinnamon or cardamom
2 tablespoons ground flaxseed or psyllium husk
    (optional – this thickens the smoothie up more)
1½ cups almond milk
Handful of ice cubes

DF	GF	V		Energy	189kcal (788kJ)
				Protein	4.6g
				Carbohydrate	19.3g (18.9g sugars)
				Fat	8.8g (0.8g sat fat)

CREAMY TROPICAL GREEN.

1 cup frozen peeled and chopped mango
1 cup peeled and chopped pineapple (ideally frozen)
1 cup spinach leaves
Juice of ½ lemon
Flesh of ½ medium avocado
1 teaspoon freshly grated ginger (optional)
½ cup coconut yoghurt or coconut milk
¾ cup cold water
Handful of ice cubes

DF	GF	V

Energy	440kcal (1841kJ)
Protein	4.8g
Carbohydrate	21.1g (19g sugars)
Fat	36.6g (8.7g sat fat)

SPICED 'PUMPKIN PIE'.

1 cup cooled steamed butternut chunks (ideally frozen)
2 pitted medjool dates
1 banana, peeled and chopped (ideally frozen)
½ teaspoon each ground cinnamon, ground ginger and mixed spice
½ cup coconut milk
3 tablespoons rolled oats
1⅓ cups cold water
Handful of ice cubes

DF	V

Energy	246kcal (1028kJ)
Protein	3.9g
Carbohydrate	41.9g (33.9g sugars)
Fat	5.2g (4.2g sat fat)

BERRY, CINNAMON AND LSA.

1 cup frozen blueberries, raspberries, boysenberries
    or strawberries (or a mix)
2 tablespoons smooth nut butter (e.g. peanut, cashew, almond)
2 tablespoons ground LSA
½ teaspoon ground cinnamon
1½ cups milk of your choice (e.g. cows, almond, rice, soy)
Handful of ice cubes

DF	GF	V

Energy	211kcal (882kJ)
Protein	12g
Carbohydrate	14.5g (12.8g sugars)
Fat	11.3g (1.5g sat fat)

Makes:	14 portions (1 bliss ball per portion)
Prep time:	10 minutes

1 cup raw cashew nuts

¼ cup shredded or desiccated coconut, plus 3–4 tablespoons extra to coat

Good pinch of Himalayan or flaky sea salt

5 pitted medjool dates (or 12 pitted dried dates, soaked in hot water for at least 5 minutes)

1 tablespoon tahini

1 tablespoon maple syrup

¼ teaspoon vanilla bean paste or extract

1 tablespoon water (if using soaked dates, omit water)

These bliss balls have a delightful caramelly flavour thanks to the combination of dates, tahini and vanilla. A little orange or lemon zest, or ground cinnamon, are also delicious additions.

1. Combine cashew nuts, coconut and salt in a food processor and blend for 30–60 seconds, until mixture is crumbly.

2. If using soaked dates, squeeze gently to remove excess liquid. Add all remaining ingredients to food processor and blend for a further 1–2 minutes, until mixture is well combined and sticky.

3. Using a tablespoon as a measure and wet hands, roll mixture into balls then roll balls in coconut to coat. Place in fridge for an hour or so to set. Keep in an airtight container in the fridge for 1–2 weeks, or in an airtight container or resealable bag in the freezer for up to 2 months.

DF	GF	V	

Energy	115kcal (480kJ)
Protein	2.5g
Carbohydrate	7.6g (6.2g sugars)
Fat	7.9g (2.7g sat fat)

HUMMUS.

Hummus is an awesome high-protein, high-fibre snack that's filling and delicious. Making your own (which takes all of 5–10 minutes) means your hummus will contain much less sodium than store-bought (and no preservatives or additives), plus you can flavour it as you like!

AVOCADO HUMMUS WITH SPINACH, LEMON AND CHILLI.

Makes:	6 portions (⅓ cup per portion)
Prep time:	10 minutes

A handful of baby spinach leaves
1 x 400g can chickpeas,
    rinsed and drained
1 clove garlic, crushed
1 tablespoon tahini
2 tablespoons lemon juice
Flesh of ½ large or 1 small avocado
Zest of ½ lemon
1 tablespoon thinly sliced red
    chilli (optional)

To serve
Superseed Crackers (see
    page 233) or store-bought
    wholegrain crackers
Vegetable sticks

Bring a half kettle of water to the boil.

1. Place the spinach leaves in a small bowl and pour over boiling water to cover, toss the leaves until wilted and bright green, then drain and set aside to cool.

2. Place chickpeas, garlic, tahini and lemon juice in a food processor or blender and blitz until well mixed. Add the wilted spinach, avocado and 2–3 tablespoons water, blitz until smooth and creamy (add a little more water if needed) then season to taste with salt and pepper.

3. Spoon avocado hummus into a serving dish and top with lemon zest and chilli (if using).

Serve with crackers or vegetable sticks for dipping.

DF | GF | V

Energy	290kcal (1213kJ)
Protein	9.4g
Carbohydrate	15.2g (2.3g sugars)
Fat	20.9g (2.7g sat fat)

Makes:	6 portions (⅓ cup per portion)
Prep time:	15 minutes
Cook time:	20 minutes

¼ head cauliflower
1 teaspoon olive oil
1 teaspoon each ground cumin
    and ground turmeric
2 cloves garlic, peeled and cut
    in half
1 x 400g can chickpeas, rinsed
    and drained
1 tablespoon tahini
2 tablespoons lemon juice
1 tablespoon finely grated
    Parmesan cheese, plus extra
    to sprinkle (optional)
Chopped coriander (optional)

To serve
Superseed Crackers (see
    page 233) or store-bought
    wholegrain crackers
Vegetable sticks

Preheat the oven to 180°C and line an oven tray with baking paper.

1. Roughly cut cauliflower into even bite-sized pieces and toss in a large bowl with the olive oil, cumin, turmeric and a good pinch of salt. Arrange in a single layer on the lined tray and dot with garlic pieces. Roast for 15–20 minutes or until the cauliflower is tender and starting to turn golden.

2. Place chickpeas, roasted cauliflower and garlic, tahini, a good pinch of salt and lemon juice in a blender or food processor and blitz well until smooth and creamy. Stir in Parmesan (if using) and then spoon into a serving dish and scatter with extra Parmesan and coriander (if using).

Serve with crackers or vegetable sticks for dipping.

GF   V   DF (omit cheese)

Energy	265kcal (1107kJ)
Protein	9.9g
Carbohydrate	15.9g (3.3g sugars)
Fat	17.5g (2.4g sat fat)

ROAST PUMPKIN HUMMUS WITH SMOKY TOASTED SEEDS.

Makes:	6 portions (⅓ cup per portion)
Prep time:	10 minutes

1 x 400g can chickpeas, rinsed
   and drained
2 cloves garlic, crushed
1 tablespoon tahini
¼ teaspoon each smoked
   paprika and ground cumin
2 tablespoons lemon juice
½ cup roasted mashed pumpkin
   or orange kumara
1 teaspoon each pumpkin
   seeds, linseeds and
   sunflower seeds

To serve
Superseed Crackers (see
   page 233) or store-bought
   wholegrain crackers
Vegetable sticks

1. Combine chickpeas, garlic, tahini, spices, lemon juice and a good pinch of salt in a food processor or blender and blitz until well mixed.

2. Add mashed pumpkin/kumara and 2–3 tablespoons of water and blitz again until smooth and creamy (add a little more water if needed). Season to taste with salt and pepper, spoon into a serving dish and chill while toasting the seeds.

3. Toast seeds in a small fry-pan on low-to-medium heat, stirring until the seeds start to toast and pop. Remove from the pan and spoon over the hummus.

Serve with crackers or vegetable sticks for dipping.

DF	GF	V

Energy	276kcal (1152kJ)
Protein	10.0g
Carbohydrate	16.3g (2.5g sugars)
Fat	18.6g (2.5g sat fat)

Makes:	1 portion
Prep time:	5–10 minutes

1 teaspoon miso paste
1 cup boiling water
1–2 tablespoons finely
  diced firm tofu
A small handful of finely
  chopped greens (e.g.
  spinach, silverbeet)
Pinch of dried seaweed
  (optional)
½ spring onion, thinly sliced

Salty, savoury, warming and nourishing, a cup of miso soup makes a great quick fix to get you through to the next meal – especially on those chilly days!

1. Place miso paste in a mug and pour in boiling water. Whisk with a fork until miso has dissolved and there are no lumps.
2. Stir in tofu, greens, seaweed (if using) and spring onion. It's best served fresh, so drink while hot. If the miso settles a bit while it sits, just stir it up again.

DF	V	GF (use GF miso)

Energy	56kcal (232kJ)
Protein	4.2g
Carbohydrate	3.6g (3.0g sugars)
Fat	2.4g (0.2g sat fat)

POPCORN.

Popcorn makes a tasty snack and you can get creative with how you flavour it. It's best eaten freshly made; however, if you want it for a snack for later it can be stored in a plastic resealable bag or airtight container for up to 3 days – just crisp it up in a 200°C oven for about 4 minutes. You need 2½ tablespoons of popping corn (popcorn kernels) to get 4 cups of freshly popped corn – follow the instructions on the packet.

Makes:	2 portions
Prep time:	5 minutes
Cook time:	5 minutes

4 cups freshly popped corn
3 tablespoons maple syrup
½ teaspoon flaky sea salt
2 tablespoons finely
    chopped pistachios

Preheat the oven to 180°C and line an oven tray with baking paper.

1. In a large bowl toss the popcorn with the maple syrup, salt and pistachios until well coated. Spread out on the lined tray in a single layer and bake for 3–4 minutes until golden and starting to caramelise. Allow to cool for a few minutes to crisp before eating or cool completely before storing in an airtight container.

DF	GF	V

Energy	186kcal (778kJ)
Protein	4.2g
Carbohydrate	29.2g (18.2g sugars)
Fat	5.2g (0.6g sat fat)

LEMON AND ROSEMARY POPCORN.

Makes:	2 portions
Prep time:	5 minutes

1 tablespoon finely grated
    lemon zest
½ teaspoon flaky sea salt
1 tablespoon very finely
    chopped rosemary leaves
4 cups freshly popped corn
2 teaspoons melted butter or
    olive oil, to drizzle

1. Combine lemon zest, salt and rosemary in a bowl and mix well. In a large bowl combine the hot popped corn with the lemon and rosemary salt and melted butter or olive oil. Transfer to a serving bowl. Eat while still hot, or leave to cool completely before storing in an airtight container.

V	GF	DF (use olive oil)

Energy	107kcal (448kJ)
Protein	2.8g
Carbohydrate	11.2g (0.3g sugars)
Fat	5.1g (2.8g sat fat)

Makes:	2 portions
Prep time:	5 minutes
Cook time:	5 minutes

2 tablespoon Sriracha chilli
   sauce, Tabasco hot sauce or
   chipotle sauce
¼ teaspoon mustard powder
½ teaspoon flaky sea salt
4 cups freshly popped corn
3 tablespoons finely grated
   hard cheese (e.g. Parmesan
   or vintage cheddar)

Preheat the oven to 180°C and line a large oven tray with baking paper.

1. Combine sauce, mustard powder and salt in a small bowl and mix well. Place popped corn in a large bowl and drizzle with the spicy sauce, tossing well to coat evenly. Arrange in an single layer on the lined tray and sprinkle over cheese.

2. Bake for 3–4 minutes or until the cheese has melted and the popcorn is starting to colour. Cool for a few minutes to crisp the popcorn up before eating, or allow to cool completely before storing in an airtight container.

GF | V

Energy	110kcal (458kJ)
Protein	1.5g
Carbohydrate	13.0g (1.5g sugars)
Fat	3.0g (1.5g sat fat)

COCONUT AND SWEET SPICED POPCORN.

Makes:	2 portions
Prep time:	10 minutes
Cook time:	5 minutes

1 teaspoon coconut sugar
1 teaspoon each ground
   cardamom and ground
   cinnamon
½ teaspoon flaky sea salt
1 tablespoon coconut oil
2½ tablespoons popping corn

1. Combine coconut sugar, cardamom, cinnamon and salt in a jar and shake well. Set aside.

2. Heat coconut oil in a large heavy-based pot (with a good fitting lid) on medium heat for a minute or so until melted and starting to swirl around. Add one corn kernel and wait till it pops then remove, add the remaining popping corn and place lid on top.

3. Shake pot occasionally whilst the corn is popping and when the popping slows remove from the heat. Sprinkle with the sugar and spice mix and toss until evenly coated. Eat while still hot or allow to cool completely before storing in an airtight container.

DF | GF | V

Energy	137kcal (573kJ)
Protein	2.0g
Carbohydrate	15.2g (2.4g sugars)
Fat	7.5g (6.0g sat fat)

Makes:	2 portions
Prep time:	5 minutes

2 tablespoons smooth nut
butter (e.g. peanut, almond
or cashew butter)
2 tablespoons hot water
4 cups freshly popped corn
½ teaspoon flaky sea salt

1. Place nut butter in a mug and add boiling water, stirring until it becomes runny and pourable. Place hot popped corn in a large bowl and drizzle over the warm nut butter. Season with salt, toss well and eat while still warm.

DF	GF	V

Energy	138kcal (578kJ)
Protein	6.1g
Carbohydrate	11.8g (0.5g sugars)
Fat	6.6g (1.1g sat fat)

Makes:	5 portions
Prep time:	15 minutes
Cook time:	1–2 minutes

3 tablespoons extra-virgin
   olive oil, plus extra to serve
2 cloves garlic, finely chopped
Zest of ½ lemon
400g white beans (e.g. cannellini),
   rinsed and drained
1 teaspoon finely chopped thyme
50g finely crumbled feta
Juice of 1 lemon

To serve
vegetable sticks
½ teaspoon extra-virgin olive oil
Squeeze of lemon juice
Strips of lemon zest (optional)
Superseed Crackers (see page
   233) or store-bought
   wholegrain crackers

This moreish bean dip is a delicious way to get some extra fibre into your day, whether you have it on crackers or with veggie sticks as a snack, or on toast or in a wrap for lunch.

1. Heat olive oil in a small fry-pan and sizzle garlic for 30–60 seconds until starting to brown. Add lemon zest, let it sizzle for a few seconds then turn off heat.

2. Tip garlic and lemon oil into food processor with beans, thyme, feta, lemon juice and a good pinch of salt. Blend until smooth. You may need to stir or scrape down the sides of the blender/food processor a few times during blending to make sure everything gets incorporated. Taste and season with a little more lemon juice and salt, if required.

3. Toss vegetable sticks with extra-virgin olive oil, lemon juice and a pinch of sea salt.

Spoon dip into a bowl, drizzle with a little extra-virgin olive oil and grind over black pepper. Scatter with lemon zest (if using). Serve with crackers and vegetable sticks for dipping.

GF | V

Energy	288kcal (1204kJ)
Protein	9.1g
Carbohydrate	14.7g (2.0g sugars)
Fat	20.7g (4.6g sat fat)

Makes:	12 portions (1 muffin per portion)
Prep time:	15 minutes
Cook time:	25 minutes

½ cup GF or wholemeal flour
½ cup ground almonds
⅓ cup desiccated coconut
1½ teaspoons baking powder
¼ teaspoon salt
2 teaspoons ground cinnamon
or mixed spice
1 cup bran flakes or wheat bran
3 tablespoons runny honey or
maple syrup
¼ cup oil (e.g. melted coconut oil
or grapeseed oil)
1 cup mashed very ripe banana
(about 2 large bananas)
1 teaspoon vanilla essence
or extract
2 free-range eggs
½ cup unsweetened natural
yoghurt or coconut yoghurt
1 level teaspoon baking soda
1 cup fresh, frozen or canned
fruit (e.g. diced apple,
feijoa, peaches, pear,
whole blueberries/
raspberries)*
Finely grated zest of 1 orange
or lemon
2 tablespoons rolled oats
(optional)
1 tablespoon coconut sugar
(optional)

High-fibre bran muffins are an excellent snack to have on hand, and these ones are light, moist, fruity and delicious. You can add whatever fruit you like to this basic recipe so you can change your muffin flavour from week to week. See over the page for ideas.

Preheat oven to 190°C. Line a medium 12-hole muffin tin with paper cases.

1. Mix flour, ground almonds, coconut, baking powder, salt, cinnamon/mixed spice and bran flakes/wheat bran in a medium bowl.

2. In a large mixing bowl, whisk honey/maple syrup, oil, banana, vanilla, eggs, yoghurt and baking soda together until well combined. Stir through fruit and zest.

3. Add flour mixture to the wet mixture and stir together until just combined, being careful not to overmix; it's fine if it's a little lumpy (this generally gives lighter muffins). Set mixture aside for a few minutes (in this time it will thicken slightly).

4. Spoon mixture into paper cases, dividing equally and being careful not to over-fill. Mix oats and sugar together (if using) and sprinkle over the top. Bake for 22–25 minutes until muffins are deep golden and they spring back when lightly pressed in the centre. Remove from oven and leave to stand in the tin for 5 minutes before transferring to a wire rack to cool. Allow to cool completely before storing in an airtight container in the fridge for up to 1 week or freeze in an airtight container or resealable bags for up to 2 months. Nice warmed up, with a cuppa!

*See flavour options over the page.

Tip: If using frozen or canned fruit, make sure it is defrosted and well drained.

Energy	178kcal (743kJ)
Protein	4.4g
Carbohydrate	17.9g (11.3g sugars)
Fat	9.0g (1.9g sat fat)

— *Peach, blueberry and orange* Use ½ cup diced fresh or canned and drained peaches, ½ cup fresh or frozen and thawed blueberries and orange zest.

— *Apple, date and spice* Use mixed spice rather than cinnamon and 1 cup peeled diced apple and ¼ cup finely chopped dates.

— *Feijoa and ginger* Use 1 cup diced feijoa and replace 1 teaspoon of the cinnamon/mixed spice with ground ginger.

— *Lemon and raspberry* Use 1 cup fresh or frozen and thawed raspberries and lemon zest.

— *Plum and spice* Use mixed spice rather than cinnamon and 1 cup diced fresh or canned and drained plums.

— *Pear, date and ginger* Use 1 cup peeled and diced pear, ¼ cup finely chopped dates and replace 1 teaspoon of the cinnamon/mixed spice with ground ginger.

Makes:	2 portions
Prep time:	5 minutes

1½ cups frozen raspberries, strawberries, mango, banana, pineapple or other chopped fruit, e.g. feijoa or persimmon
½ cup unsweetened natural yoghurt or coconut yoghurt
½ teaspoon vanilla extract or rosewater
5 mint or basil leaves (optional)

One of the best and quickest snacks you can have, especially in the warmer months. Go crazy with different fruit flavours!

1. Place everything in a food processor and blitz, scraping down the sides as necessary to ensure everything is incorporated, until smooth and just like frozen yoghurt! Scoop into bowls or glasses and enjoy!

| V | GF | DF (use coconut yoghurt) |

Energy	63kcal (262kJ)
Protein	4.1g
Carbohydrate	7.7g (7.2g sugars)
Fat	0.8g (0.2g sat fat)

Making your own crispy crackers for snacks is easy, and they'll be full of so much goodness with the amount of seeds packed into them. Then load them up with your favourite nutritious toppings for a great snack or light meal.

Makes:	12 portions (24 crackers, 2 per portion)
Prep time:	10 minutes
Cook time:	40–50 minutes

½ cup pumpkin seeds
½ cup sunflower seeds
¼ cup sesame seeds
1 tablespoon very finely chopped rosemary and/or thyme
½ teaspoon garlic powder or 1 small clove garlic, finely minced
1 cup ground almonds
½ teaspoon salt
1 tablespoon psyllium husk
2 tablespoons water
¼ cup boiling water
2 tablespoons olive oil, plus 2 teaspoons extra, for brushing

Preheat oven to 160°C. Bring a quarter kettle of water to the boil.

1. Place pumpkin seeds, sunflower seeds, sesame seeds, herbs, garlic powder/garlic, ground almonds and salt in a large mixing bowl and stir to combine.

2. In a small bowl, mix psyllium husk with the 2 tablespoons water for 30 seconds until thickened, then whisk in boiling water and olive oil.

3. Add psyllium husk mixture to dry mixture and stir until evenly combined and it forms a sticky dough. Divide and mould dough into two balls.

4. Place a large piece of baking paper (about the size of an oven tray) on a clean flat surface and place one ball of dough on it. Use a rolling pin to roll dough out to 0.5cm thick. The dough will be very malleable, so you can shape it into a rectangle if you like, or leave it more free-form. And don't worry if any little tears form, just push the dough back together to patch it up – easy peasy!

5. Lift edges of baking paper and transfer rolled-out dough to an oven tray. Brush lightly with 1 teaspoon olive oil and sprinkle with a good pinch of flaky sea salt. Bake for 20–23 minutes or until firm, golden around the edges and crispy. Keep an eye on the crackers in the last 5 minutes of cooking time to ensure they don't brown too quickly.

Lift baking paper to transfer crackers from tray to a chopping board and, while warm, use a large sharp knife to cut into 12 roughly evenly sized pieces. Repeat with remaining dough. Leave to cool completely before storing in an airtight container.

Topping ideas:
— Avocado, tomato, sea salt and cracked black pepper
— Ricotta, cucumber, smoked salmon and dill
— Hummus, cucumber and sauerkraut or pickled red onion
— Edamame beans smashed with lemon juice and a little crumbled feta

DF GF V

Energy	161kcal (671kJ)
Protein	5.0g
Carbohydrate	4.0g (0.6g sugars)
Fat	14.0g (1.8g sat fat)

PUMPKIN KUMARA MASH.

Makes:	4 portions
Prep time:	10 minutes
Cook time:	15 minutes

300g kumara (red, gold or
   orange), peeled and chopped
300g peeled butternut or
   pumpkin, chopped
1 tablespoon butter or
   extra-virgin olive oil

1. Place kumara, butternut/pumpkin, and a good pinch of salt in a pot, cover with water and bring to the boil. Cook for 10-12 minutes or until tender.
2. Drain well, tip back into pot and place back on low heat for a few minutes – this will help the kumara and butternut to dry out a little.
3. Mash with butter/extra-virgin olive oil, and season to taste with salt and pepper.

V	GF	DF (use oil)

Energy	128kcal (534kJ)
Protein	1.7g
Carbohydrate	20.4g (10.7g sugars)
Fat	3.8g (2.3g sat fat)

CAULIFLOWER PARSLEY MASH.

Makes:	4 portions
Prep time:	10 minutes
Cook time:	15 minutes

500g cauliflower, chopped
300g agria potatoes, peeled
   and chopped
1 tablespoon butter or extra-
   virgin olive oil
½ small clove garlic,
   finely minced
¼–½ cup finely chopped
   parsley

A great way to have a creamy mash with half the calories and more vegetable goodness!

1. Place cauliflower, potato and a good pinch of salt in a pot, cover with water and bring to the boil. Cook for 10–12 minutes or until tender.
2. Drain well, tip back into pot and place back on low heat for a few minutes – this will help the potato and cauliflower to dry out a little.
3. Mash with butter/oil, garlic, parsley, and season to taste with salt and pepper.

V	GF	DF (use oil)

Energy	127kcal (530kJ)
Protein	4.8g
Carbohydrate	16.5g (4.4g sugars)
Fat	3.9g (0.7g sat fat)

Makes:	12 portions (1½ cups, 2 tablespoons per portion)
Prep time:	10 minutes
Cook time:	20 minutes

1 small beetroot (about 90g), peeled and chopped
1 small carrot (about 80g), peeled and chopped
2 teaspoons maple syrup
3 teaspoons olive oil
1 onion, diced
1 cup tomato passata or tomato purée
3 tablespoons tomato paste
1½ tablespoons malt vinegar (or white wine or apple cider vinegar for GF)
1¼ teaspoons salt
1 tablespoon maple syrup
2 teaspoons Worcestershire sauce
⅛ teaspoon ground cloves
Good pinch of dried oregano
¼ teaspoon smoked paprika

Most people love a squirt of tomato sauce with their chips, but unfortunately commercial versions can be chock-full of added sugar and salt. So here's our clever, delicious recipe that sneaks in roasted vegetables as the main sweetener!

Preheat oven to 200°C. Line an oven try with baking paper.

1. Toss beetroot and carrot with maple syrup and 2 teaspoons of the olive oil on prepared tray. Season with salt and roast for about 20 minutes or until soft and caramelised.

2. Heat remaining 1 teaspoon olive oil in a medium pot on medium heat. Cook onion, with a pinch of salt, for a few minutes until soft and starting to turn a little golden. Stir in tomato passata/purée and tomato paste and simmer, stirring frequently, for about 5 minutes.

3. Transfer roasted vegetables, tomato mixture and all remaining ingredients to a blender and blend until very smooth. Taste and adjust seasoning. Will keep in the fridge for up to 10 days or can be frozen for months.

DF | V | GF (use GF vinegar and Worcestershire)

Energy 34kcal (143kJ)
Protein 0.7g
Carbohydrate 4.6g (3.6g sugars)
Fat 1.2g (0.2g sat fat)

Makes:	4 portions
Prep time:	15 minutes

Herby dressing
½ cup unsweetened natural
   Greek yoghurt
Juice of ½ lemon
½ teaspoon wholegrain or
   Dijon mustard
¼ teaspoon flaky sea salt
2 tablespoons chopped dill
2–3 tablespoons chopped
   mint leaves
2 tablespoons chopped
   flat-leaf parsley

Slaw
5 cups shredded purple and/or
   green cabbage (about ½
   small head cabbage)
1 carrot, peeled and shredded
   or coarsely grated
2 spring onions, thinly sliced

Simple, fresh and crunchy with a fresh herb and yoghurt dressing.

1. To make the dressing, blitz all ingredients in a food processor or blender until almost smooth and pale green. If you do not have a food processor or blender, you can simply whisk together the liquid ingredients and flaky sea salt until smooth, then very finely chop the herbs and stir through. Season to taste with salt and pepper.
2. Place cabbage, carrot and spring onion in a large bowl. Add dressing just before serving and toss until evenly coated. Serve immediately.

GF   V

Energy	51kcal (213kJ)
Protein	4.1g
Carbohydrate	5.1g (4.8g sugars)
Fat	0.8g (0.3g sat fat)

Makes:	4 portions
Prep time:	10 minutes
Cook time:	5-15 minutes

1 head cauliflower (about
    750–800g including stem),
    cut into florets
1 tablespoon butter or extra-
    virgin olive oil
¼–½ cup chopped fresh parsley
    or coriander (optional)
Pinch of finely grated lemon
    zest (optional)

Cauliflower rice is awesome – light, fluffy and the texture of cooked rice, it makes the perfect low-calorie, low-carb side to lots of dishes.

1. Place cauliflower florets in a food processor and briefly blitz until it resembles the texture of rice or couscous. You may have to do this in batches to avoid overcrowding the food processor. If you don't have a food processor, you can either finely chop the cauliflower or coarsely grate it.

2. Transfer to a large glass or microwavable bowl and microwave on high for a few minutes – this steams the cauliflower and evaporates moisture to make it extra fluffy. If you don't have a microwave, spread cauliflower out on an oven tray lined with baking paper and bake in a 200°C oven for 10–15 minutes until just tender and fluffy.

3. Toss hot cauliflower rice with butter/extra-virgin olive oil, herbs and lemon zest (if using), and season to taste with a little salt and pepper.

V GF DF (use oil)

Energy	92kcal (385kJ)
Protein	4.6g
Carbohydrate	7.7g (6.7g sugars)
Fat	4.0g (0.7g sat fat)

Makes:	4 portions
Prep time:	10 minutes
Cook time:	30-40 minutes

3 large or 4 medium parsnips,
  scrubbed (leave skin on)
3 large or 4 medium carrots,
  scrubbed (leave skin on)
1 tablespoon olive oil
2 teaspoons maple syrup
½ teaspoon salt

A scrumptious way to eat your vegetables, especially when served with our refined sugar-free Tomato Sauce (see page 237)!

Preheat oven to 220°C. Line a large oven tray with baking paper.

1. Cut vegetables into 1cm-thick wedges or chips. Toss with olive oil, maple syrup and salt in lined tray and spread out in a single layer.

2. Bake for 30-40 minutes, turning once or twice during cooking, until golden.

DF	GF	V

Energy	157kcal (656kJ)
Protein	3.4g
Carbohydrate	23.9g (19.6g sugars)
Fat	4.0g (0.7g sat fat)

Makes:	1¼ cups (1 tablespoon per portion)
Prep time:	10 minutes
Cook time:	5–10 minutes

1½ teaspoons coriander seeds
1½ teaspoons cumin seeds
1 teaspoon fennel seeds
1 teaspoon curry powder
2 teaspoons olive oil
2 cloves garlic, finely chopped
Zest of ½ lemon
1 teaspoon finely chopped
    rosemary leaves
½ cup chopped raw macadamias
½ cup chopped raw cashew nuts
½ teaspoon smoked paprika
1 teaspoon flaky sea salt
Good pinch of ground chilli or
    chilli flakes (optional)
1 tablespoon maple syrup

This nut scatter is perfect for sprinkling over salads for extra flavour and texture. There's only one problem with it – it's seriously addictive!

1. Crush coriander, cumin and fennel seeds in a spice grinder or mortar and pestle and mix with curry powder.
2. Heat olive oil in a medium fry-pan on low-medium heat. Add garlic, spice mixture, lemon zest and rosemary, and cook, stirring, for 1–2 minutes until fragrant.
3. Add nuts and continue cooking, stirring to coat everything nice and evenly, for a few minutes to lightly toast the nuts.
4. Add smoked paprika, sea salt and chilli (if using) and maple syrup – the maple syrup will bubble away. Stir to coat everything and keep cooking for a further 1 minute or so. Turn off heat and transfer to a dish or bowl to cool completely and go crunchy before storing. Store in an airtight container in the fridge for up to 4 weeks.

DF | GF | V

Energy	58kcal (244kJ)
Protein	1.1g
Carbohydrate	1.7g (1.1g sugars)
Fat	5.2g (0.8g sat fat)

Makes:	4 portions
Prep time:	5–10 minutes
Cook time:	5 minutes

1 teaspoon olive oil
4 cups vegetables (e.g. broccoli
   or cauliflower cut into florets,
   peeled and sliced carrots,
   trimmed green beans or
   asparagus)
4 handfuls leafy greens
   (e.g. spinach, silverbeet,
   collard greens, kale or
   sliced cabbage)
Squeeze of lemon juice (optional)

Cut the vegetables (apart from the leafy greens) into roughly the same sized pieces so they cook evenly.

1. Heat olive oil in a large fry-pan on medium heat. Add vegetables and cook, stirring often, for a few minutes until brightly coloured and just-tender. Add leafy greens and 1–2 tablespoons of water and cover with a lid to help vegetables steam and cook through. Squeeze over lemon juice (if using) before serving.

| DF | GF | V |

Energy	46kcal (192kJ)
Protein	3.3g
Carbohydrate	3.1g (2.9g sugars)
Fat	1.6g (0.2g sat fat)

Makes:	1 portion (but increase quantity as required)
Prep time:	3 minutes

1 large handful of leafy greens
   (e.g. rocket, mesclun,
   lettuce, mizuna, watercress,
   baby spinach, or a mixture)
½ teaspoon extra-virgin olive oil
Squeeze of lemon juice

Dressing your salad greens with a little extra-virgin olive oil, a squeeze of lemon juice and a pinch of salt makes all the difference.

1. Gently toss leafy greens with olive oil, a squeeze of lemon juice and a pinch of flaky sea salt just before serving.

DF   GF   V

Energy   28kcal (115kJ)
Protein   1.0g
Carbohydrate 0.1g (0.1g sugars)
Fat   2.4g (0.4g sat fat)

Makes:	1 loaf (24 slices, 2 slices per portion)
Prep time:	10 minutes
Cook time:	1 hour

¾ cup sunflower seeds
½ cup flaxseeds (linseeds)
½ cup pumpkin seeds
½ cup GF flour
½ cup ground almonds
2 tablespoons chia seeds
¼ cup psyllium husk
1 teaspoon salt
1½ cups boiling water
3 tablespoons melted
   coconut oil or butter
1 tablespoon honey or
   maple syrup

This is a fantastic gluten-free bread recipe inspired by the original 'Life-changing loaf' recipe. Because of the amount of seeds in it, it is a dense bread so you only need a thin slice. Load one or two slices up with delicious nutritious toppings and you've got a great snack or lunch. For a loaf that's not gluten-free, you can replace the GF flour and ground almonds with 1 cup of wholemeal flour or oat flour (oats blitzed in a food processor until a flour forms).

Preheat oven to 170°C. Lightly grease a loaf tin.

1. In a large mixing bowl, mix seeds, flour, ground almonds, chia seeds, psyllium husks and salt together.

2. In a jug or another bowl, mix boiling water with coconut oil and honey/maple syrup until coconut oil is melted. Add to dry ingredients and stir until well combined and dough is very thick. (Note: if using GF flour and ground almonds, the batter will be much wetter than if using wholemeal/oat flour).

3. Spoon mixture into loaf tin and smooth out the top. Bake for 20 minutes on the middle rack of the oven.

4. Remove bread from oven and tip out onto an oven tray. Return to oven to bake for a further 40–45 minutes until golden. The loaf is ready when tapped and it sounds hollow. Let the bread completely cool before slicing (this part is essential, so don't be tempted to cut into it straight away!).

Tip: psyllium husk is a type of dietary fibre that swells when mixed with water and works well as a natural thickener; and binder in many gluten-free baking recipes. Find it in the health section.

GF | V | DF (use coconut oil)

Energy	235kcal (982kJ)
Protein	7.4g
Carbohydrate	10.1g (2.0g sugars)
Fat	17.8g (4.6g sat fat)

SAUCES, MARINADES & DRESSINGS.

A good spice mix, marinade or dressing can transform an ordinary dish into something ultra-delicious. The great thing is they're a simple way to add flavour without copious amounts of fat, salt or sugar. The pastes will keep in the fridge for up to 2 weeks or can be frozen. Spice mixes will keep in a small airtight jar for weeks. Dressings will keep in a clean jar in the fridge for up to 1 week.

PIZZA SAUCE.

Tip 1 x 400g can crushed tomatoes into a
fry-pan. Stir in 2 tablespoons tomato paste, 1
teaspoon coconut or brown sugar, ½ teaspoon
dried mixed herbs and 2 teaspoons extra-
virgin olive oil. Simmer, stirring often, for
about 10 minutes until sauce is thick and the
consistency of chutney. Season to taste with salt
and pepper. Allow to cool before using. Makes
just over 1 cup (enough for 4 pizza bases).

DF | V | GF

MEXICAN SEASONING.

Mix together 1 teaspoon paprika, 1 teaspoon
smoked paprika, 1 teaspoon ground cumin,
1 teaspoon ground coriander, 1 teaspoon dried
oregano or mixed herbs, ¼ teaspoon ground
chilli or cayenne pepper and ½ teaspoon each
onion and garlic powder (optional) in a small
bowl. Makes 2 tablespoons.

DF | V | GF

ASIAN DRESSING.

Place 3 tablespoons soy sauce, 3 tablespoons
freshly squeezed lemon or lime juice, 1½
tablespoons sweet chilli sauce or runny honey,
2 teaspoons rice vinegar and ½ teaspoon
sesame oil (optional) in a jar, screw lid on tight
and shake to mix all ingredients together.
Makes ½ cup.

DF | V | GF (use GF soy sauce)

TANDOORI PASTE.

Mix together 1 tablespoon ground cumin,
2 teaspoons ground coriander, 1 tablespoon
smoked paprika, 1 teaspoon ground turmeric,
½–1 teaspoon ground chilli, 1 teaspoon
finely minced/grated fresh ginger, 2 cloves
minced garlic, 2 tablespoons tomato paste,
1 teaspoon salt and 2 tablespoons natural
yoghurt. Makes ½ cup.

GF | V | DF (use coconut yoghurt)

KAFFIR LIME LEAF, LEMONGRASS OR CHILLI DRESSING.

Make Asian Dressing (see above) and add 1–2
finely shredded or chopped kaffir lime leaves
(tough stems removed first), 2 teaspoons finely
chopped lemongrass or 1 small finely chopped
chilli for extra flavour.

DF | V | GF (use GF soy sauce)

HONEY MUSTARD DRESSING.

Place 2 teaspoons wholegrain mustard,
2 teaspoons runny honey, 2 tablespoons
apple cider vinegar or juice of 1 lemon, and
1½ tablespoons extra-virgin olive oil in a
jar, screw lid on tight and shake to mix all
ingredients together. Season with salt and
pepper. Makes ⅓ cup.

DF | V | GF

CHIMICHURRI.

In a bowl, mix together ⅓ cup finely chopped flat-leaf parsley, ⅓ cup finely chopped mint leaves, 3 tablespoons extra-virgin olive oil, 4 tablespoons red wine vinegar, 2–3 small cloves garlic, finely minced, ½ teaspoon honey, ¾ teaspoon dried oregano and ½–1 teaspoon chilli flakes. Season to taste with salt and set aside for at least 15 minutes to allow flavours to meld together. Makes ¾ cup.

DF | V | GF

HARISSA PASTE.

Place 3 cloves chopped garlic, 1–2 chopped red chillies, 1½ tablespoons crushed cumin seeds, 1 tablespoon crushed coriander seeds, 3–4 tablespoons olive oil, 2 tablespoons tomato paste, 1 teaspoon coconut or brown sugar, juice of ½ lemon and 1 teaspoon salt in a food processor and blitz until well combined. Makes ½ cup.

DF | V | GF

THAI GREEN CURRY PASTE.

Place ½ cup chopped coriander (roots, stalks and leaves), 4–5 whole green chillies, 1 teaspoon crushed black peppercorns, 1 peeled and chopped shallot, 1 tablespoon ground coriander, 1½ tablespoons minced or grated fresh ginger, 4 cloves chopped garlic, 2 stalks finely chopped lemongrass (tough outer leaves removed first), 3 finely chopped kaffir lime leaves (tough stems removed first), 1½ teaspoons salt, 2 tablespoons tomato paste, and 2 tablespoons oil in a food processor and blend until smooth. Heat 1 tablespoon oil in a fry-pan on medium heat and cook curry paste for a few minutes, stirring frequently until fragrant and thickened. Will keep in the fridge for up to 5 days or can be frozen for months. Makes 1 cup.

DF | V | GF

LEMONGRASS PASTE.

Place 3 stalks chopped lemongrass (tough outer leaves removed first), 2 tablespoons oil, 2½ tablespoons fish sauce or soy sauce, 2 teaspoons ground turmeric, 2 teaspoons coconut or brown sugar, 2 teaspoons chopped chilli, 2 cloves chopped garlic and 1cm peeled and chopped ginger in a small food processor and blitz until a paste forms. Alternatively pound all ingredients together in a mortar and pestle. Makes ½ cup.

DF | V | GF (use GF soy sauce)

HERB AND CASHEW PESTO.

Place 1½ cups basil leaves (and/or coriander leaves and stalks), ½ cup chopped parsley, ½ clove chopped garlic, ¼ cup cashew nuts (roasted or plain) and ¼ cup grated Parmesan cheese in a food processor and blitz to combine. With motor running, slowly drizzle in ⅓ cup extra-virgin olive oil. Season to taste with 1–2 tablespoons lemon juice, salt and pepper. Makes 1 cup (16 portions, 1 portion = 1 tablespoon). Will keep in the fridge for up to 5 days or can be frozen in a small resealable bag for up to 1 month.

V	GF	DF (omit Parmesan)

Energy	64kcal (269 kJ)
Protein	1.3g
Carbohydrate	0.6g (0.2g sugars)
Fat	6.3g (1.2g sat fat)

SWEET CHILLI SAUCE.

Heat 1 tablespoon oil in a fry pan on medium heat. Add 1 red capsicum, cored, finely diced, and cook for about 3 minutes until soft. Add 2–3 cloves garlic, minced, 2 tablespoons finely grated fresh ginger and ½ teaspoon ground turmeric, and continue cooking for 1 minute. Then add 3 large red chillies (de-seed 2 and leave 1 with seeds in for a little bit of heat), finely chopped, ⅔ cup orange juice, 3 tablespoons rice vinegar, 2½ tablespoons honey, 2 tablespoons coconut or brown sugar, juice of 1 lime, ¼ teaspoon salt and ¼ cup water. Bring to a boil and cook for about 10 minutes, stirring often, until thickened. It will continue to thicken as it cools. Store in the fridge in a clean bottle or jar for 2–3 weeks (or can be frozen). Makes 200ml (20 portions, 1 portion = 2 teaspoons).

DF	V	GF (use GF soy sauce)

Energy	22 kcal (94 kJ)
Protein	0.2g
Carbohydrate	3.8g (3.5g sugars)
Fat	0.7g (0.1g sat fat)

chapter six—

sweets

- *A piece of fruit is the most nutritious sweet treat,* perfectly packaged up with vitamins, minerals, fibre and water. However, if you feel like a little something more in the sweet treat department, this section has got lots of great recipes. Overall, they're lower in sugar and use less refined sugars. Rather, they use more fresh and dried fruit, spices and citrus for flavour. They also use more nutritious ingredients, like nuts, seeds and coconut, instead of plain white flours, so many have ended up being gluten-free and lower GI.

- *Unrefined and refined sugars* are equally calorific and raise blood sugar levels, so the bottom line is that both should only be eaten in very small quantities. However, the difference with unrefined sweeteners such as honey or pure maple syrup is that you do at least get some vitamins and minerals (but still not enough to justify eating much!).

- *So all in all, make sure you keep sweet treats as just that – treats,* and only have them once or twice a week. And on the odd special occasion, feel free to have something more indulgent (and don't feel guilty about it!) – remember, it's what you do most of the time that counts, not what happens now and again. Enjoy!

Makes: 8 portions

2 cups chopped fresh, peeled
  peaches or canned (and
  drained) peaches in juice
2 tablespoons liquid honey
¾ cup unsweetened natural
  yoghurt or coconut yoghurt
1 teaspoon vanilla bean paste
  or extract
½ cup milk e.g. (cows, almond,
  rice, soy)

1. Blitz peaches and 1 tablespoon of the honey in a blender or food processor until a smooth purée. Pour into a jug (this will make it easier to pour into moulds).

2. Add yoghurt, milk, vanilla and remaining 1 tablespoon honey into empty blender (don't bother washing it) and blitz briefly until just combined and pour into a jug.

3. Pour half of the yoghurt mixture into 8 x 80–100ml ice-block moulds, dividing equally, then freeze for about 30 minutes until semi-solid. Top up ice-block moulds with peach and honey purée, dividing equally, then freeze for about 30 minutes until semi-solid. Finally, top up with remaining yoghurt mixture, return to freezer for another 30 minutes or so before inserting ice-block sticks. Freeze layered ice-blocks for at least 8 hours/overnight or until frozen solid.

| V | GF | DF (use coconut yoghurt and DF milk) |

Energy	56kcal (234kJ)
Protein	2.1g
Carbohydrate	10.7g (10.6g sugars)
Fat	0.3g (0.2g sat fat)

PINEAPPLE SNOW.

Makes: 8 portions

2 cups chopped ripe pineapple
  flesh (discard tough core)
  – from about ½ large ripe
  pineapple
¾ cup freshly squeezed orange
  juice
⅓ cup coconut yoghurt or
  coconut cream
½ cup coconut thread

1. Place all ingredients in a food processor and blend until smooth.

2. Pour into a jug and pour into 8 x 80–100ml ice-block moulds, dividing mixture equally. Freeze for about 30 minutes before inserting ice-block sticks, then continue to freeze for at least 8 hours/overnight or until frozen solid.

| V | GF | DF | |

Energy	116kcal (483kJ)
Protein	1.2g
Carbohydrate	9.5g (9.1g sugars)
Fat	7.8g (5.3g sat fat)

Makes: 8 portions

1 cup unsweetened natural
 yoghurt or coconut yoghurt
1 ripe banana
1 teaspoon vanilla bean paste
 or extract
¾ cup milk e.g. (cows, almond,
 rice, soy)
1 cup fresh or frozen blueberries
1 tablespoon maple syrup

1. Place all ingredients in a food processor or blender and pulse until blueberries are broken up.
2. Pour mixture into 8 x 80-100ml ice-block moulds and freeze for about 30 minutes before inserting ice-block sticks, then continue to freeze for at least 8 hours/ overnight or until frozen solid.

V	GF	DF (use coconut yoghurt and DF milk)

Energy	57kcal (238kJ)
Protein	2.5g
Carbohydrate	9.8g (9.5g sugars)
Fat	0.5g (0.3g sat fat)

MELLOW YELLOW.

Makes: 8 portions

1 cup mashed cooked pumpkin
 and/or carrot
2 cups diced ripe mango (fresh
 or frozen)
1½ cups freshly squeezed
 orange juice

1. Place all the ingredients into a blender or food processor and blitz until smooth.
2. Pour into 8 x 80–100ml ice-block moulds and freeze for about 30 minutes before inserting ice-block sticks, then continue to freeze for at least 8 hours/overnight or until frozen solid.

V	GF	DF

Energy	56kcal (232kJ)
Protein	0.7g
Carbohydrate	12g (11.4g sugars)
Fat	0.2g (0.1g sat fat)

KOMBUCHACLES.

Makes:	**8 portions**

2 cups kombucha
1–2 tablespoons liquid honey to
  sweeten
1 cup fruit e.g. berries,
  pomegranate seeds, sliced
  strawberries, diced orange or
  mandarin, kiwifruit or stone fruit

Lemon and ginger-flavoured kombucha pairs well with diced mandarin and orange, whereas hibiscus-flavoured kombucha is delicious with strawberries and pomegranate seeds.

1. Decant the kombucha into a large jug and sweeten to taste with the honey, mixing well until dissolved.
2. Arrange fruit in the base of 8 x 80–100ml ice-block moulds and top up with the kombucha, filling to three-quarters of the way up (they expand upon freezing so don't go too much higher than this). Freeze for about 30 minutes before inserting ice-block sticks, then continue to freeze for at least 8 hours/overnight or until frozen solid.

V	GF	DF	

Energy	31kcal (128kJ)
Protein	0.1g
Carbohydrate	7.4g (5.3g sugars)
Fat	0.1g (0g sat fat)

MINTY GREENS.

Makes:	**8 portions**

1½ handful baby spinach leaves
½ cup frozen peas (minted ones
  if possible)
15–20 mint leaves
½ cup roughly chopped cucumber
1 ripe banana
1½ cups diced ripe pineapple
  flesh (discard tough core)
⅔ cup coconut water or water
2 tablespoons lime or lemon juice

1. Place spinach and peas in a heat-proof bowl and pour over boiling water to cover. Leave for a few minutes then drain well and squeeze excess water out from spinach.
2. Place spinach, peas and all other remaining ingredients into a blender or food processor and whizz until smooth and bright green.
3. Pour into 8 x 80–100ml ice-block moulds and freeze for about 30 minutes before inserting ice-block sticks, then continue to freeze for at least 8 hours/overnight or until frozen solid.

V	GF	DF	

Energy	36kcal (152kJ)
Protein	0.5g
Carbohydrate	7.7g (7.4g sugars)
Fat	0.2g (0g sat fat)

Makes:	18 portions (1 cookie per portion)
Prep time:	15 minutes
Cook time:	15–20 minutes

3 tablespoons coconut oil, melted and cooled slightly

1 teaspoon vanilla extract or essence

¼ cup runny honey or maple syrup

2 free-range eggs

2¼ cups ground almonds

Finely grated zest of 1 lemon

⅓ cup shelled pistachios, finely chopped

½ cup dried apricots, roughly chopped

These fruit and nut cookies are made with a ground almond base. Perfect with your mid-morning cuppa!

Preheat oven to 160°C. Line a large oven tray with baking paper.

1. In a large bowl, combine coconut oil, vanilla, honey/maple syrup and eggs. Whisk well to combine.

2. Add remaining ingredients and stir until combined. Use wet hands (to help avoid a sticky mess) to roll tablespoons of mixture into walnut-sized balls and place on lined tray. You should get about 18 cookies. Flatten each cookie with the back of a wet fork.

3. Bake for 16–18 minutes or until light golden and cooked through.

4. Cool for 5 minutes on tray, then transfer to a wire rack to cool completely before storing in an airtight container. They'll keep in the fridge for up to a week or can be frozen and kept for a couple of months.

Energy	129kcal (540kJ)
Protein	3.9g
Carbohydrate	7.4g (5.2g sugars)
Fat	9.7g (2.6g sat fat)

Makes:	8 portions
Prep time:	15 minutes + at least 6 hours freezer time

Base

½ cup desiccated or
   shredded coconut
7–8 pitted medjool dates
   (or 15–16 normal dried dates
   soaked in boiling hot water
   for 5 minutes)
⅓ cup sunflower seeds or almonds

Filling

500g mix of frozen raspberries
   and strawberries, defrosted
¼ cup runny honey or maple syrup
1–2 teaspoons rosewater or
   vanilla bean paste or extract
1 cup cream or coconut cream
1¼ cups unsweetened natural
   Greek yoghurt or coconut
   yoghurt

This frozen ice cream/yoghurt cake is incredibly refreshing and summery, and so quick and easy to make (plus you can make it well in advance). It's a great one to make for a special occasion without wanting to blow out on dessert calories! You could use a mixture of boysenberries and blackberries instead of raspberries and strawberries to get a different berry flavour and colour.

Grease the bottom and sides of a 20–21cm round spring-form cake tin and line with baking paper.

1. To make the base, place all ingredients in a food processor and blitz until well combined and the mixture has formed a slightly sticky dough that holds together well when pinched between your fingers; if it's still a little crumbly just add 1–2 tablespoons water and blitz again. Scrape down the sides of the food processor as necessary to ensure all the ingredients are incorporated. Spread mixture over the base of prepared cake tin using the back of a spoon – it will be quite a thin layer. Place in the freezer while you make the filling.

2. Blend berries, honey/maple syrup and rosewater/vanilla until smooth. Scoop out ½ cup berry mixture and set aside in a bowl.

3. Add cream/coconut cream and yoghurt to remaining berry mixture and blend together briefly until combined and a pretty pink colour.

4. Pour filling over the base and roughly smooth out the top. Spoon reserved berry sauce over the filling and use a teaspoon or knife to create a few pretty swirls. Freeze for at least 6 hours (or overnight) until firm.

When ready to serve, remove from freezer and stand at room temperature for 10–15 minutes to slightly thaw, before releasing spring latch and removing cake from tin. Decorate with extra berries and flower petals if you like. Use a large, sharp knife to cut into portions.

GF	V	DF (use coconut cream and coconut yoghurt)		

Energy	335kcal (1402kJ)
Protein	5.6g
Carbohydrate	25.1g (23.8g sugars)
Fat	22.8g (13.5g sat fat)

Makes:	6 portions (6 panna cotta)
Prep time:	10 minutes
Cook time:	5 minutes + at least 4 hours chilling time

Coconut oil, for greasing
¼ cup water
2½ teaspoons gelatine powder
¾ cup cream or coconut cream
¼ cup runny honey
600ml buttermilk
1 tablespoon rosewater or
    1 teaspoon vanilla extract or essence
Finely grated zest of ½ orange
Seeds of 1 pomegranate, to serve

A lovely light dessert that you can make ahead if serving to guests. While jewel-like pomegranate seeds look so beautiful, the panna cotta goes well with just about any type of fruit so feel free to serve it with whatever you have/ is in season, such as passionfruit pulp, orange or mandarin segments, sliced stone fruit, berries, etc.

Lightly grease 6 small panna cotta moulds (or use small serving glasses or tea cups, in which case you don't have to grease them).

1. Measure the water into a small jug or cup and sprinkle over the gelatine. Set aside for 5 minutes to allow the gelatine to swell.

2. Meanwhile, pour cream/coconut cream into a medium pot and stir in the honey. Heat gently on the stove top, until the honey has dissolved and the mixture has almost come to the boil (however, be careful it doesn't boil). Remove from the heat and stir in the gelatine mixture until smooth.

3. Allow cream mixture to cool, then whisk in buttermilk, rosewater/vanilla and orange zest. Pour into moulds or glasses. Chill, covered, for at least 4 hours (or overnight) until set.

4. If using moulds, unmould panna cotta (see tip below) onto little serving plates; if using glasses or tea cups, just serve as is. Scatter over pomegranate seeds just before serving.

Tip: To unmould the panna cottas, dip the base of each mould in hot water for a few seconds then prise the panna cotta away from the top edge with your fingertips or a small knife and carefully invert onto a serving plate.

GF | V

Energy 215kcal (900kJ)
Protein 5.1g
Carbohydrate 18.4g (17.3g sugars)
Fat 13.5g (8.3g sat fat)

CHOCOLATE CUSTARD WITH ORANGE AND CINNAMON PRUNES.

Makes:	4 portions
Prep time:	10 minutes
Cook time:	10 minutes

Orange and cinnamon prunes
12 pitted prunes
Zest of 1 orange
Juice of 2 oranges
2 teaspoons maple syrup
1 cinnamon stick

Chocolate custard
2 level tablespoons
    custard powder
1 free-range egg yolk
2¼ cups milk
50g dark (e.g. 70% cocoa)
    chocolate, chopped
¾ teaspoon vanilla extract
    or essence
2–3 teaspoons maple syrup

As a yummy healthy pudding, Mum used to make us chocolate custard with prunes. This version is a little more special because I've melted real dark chocolate into the custard (whereas Mum just used a bit of cocoa powder). The flavour is sensational with prunes soaked in orange and cinnamon.

1. Combine all prune ingredients in a small pot, cover and bring to a simmer. Cook, stirring often, for about 5 minutes or until prunes are fat and juicy, and syrup has reduced. Set aside.

2. To make custard, in a small pot, whisk custard powder, egg yolk and ¼ cup of the milk together until smooth. Whisk in remaining milk and bring to a gentle boil on the stove top, then reduce heat and simmer for 2 minutes, whisking frequently, until thickened. Whisk in chocolate, vanilla and maple syrup until chocolate is melted and smooth.

3. Divide custard between 4 serving glasses or bowls and top each with 3 prunes. Drizzle over any orange syrup. Serve warm straight away, or chill in the fridge to serve cold.

GF | V | DF (use DF milk and DF chocolate)

Energy	230kcal (960kJ)
Protein	7.7g
Carbohydrate	29.3g (24.8g sugars)
Fat	8.5g (4.6g sat fat)

Makes:	12 portions
Prep time:	15 minutes
Cook time:	1 hour

300–370g whole oranges or
    mandarins or tangelos (if
    using oranges, choose a
    thin-skinned variety)
¾ cup honey
250g ground almonds
4 free-range eggs, whisked well
1½ tablespoons poppy seeds
1 teaspoon baking powder

Syrup
1 tablespoon sugar or honey
2–3 tablespoons lemon or
    lime juice

This incredibly moist, fruity cake-style loaf keeps well in the
fridge for a few days (in fact, its flavour develops even more
when left overnight). It's beautiful served either warm or
cold, by itself or with Greek yoghurt.

1. Place whole citrus fruit in a medium pot and cover
    with water. Cover, bring to the boil, and simmer for about
    45 minutes or until fruit is very soft (test with the tip of
    a knife and keep an eye on the pot and top up with water
    if needed).

2. Preheat oven to 180°C. Line a standard-sized (5–6 cup
    capacity) loaf tin with baking paper. Remove the stem end
    of the fruit, then cut in half and remove any pips. Weigh
    the fruit and cut off and discard some to get 320g. Place
    whole fruit (skin, pith, flesh and all) in a food processor or
    blender with the honey and blitz until smooth.

3. Pour into a large mixing bowl and stir in ground almonds,
    eggs, poppy seeds and baking powder.

4. Pour into prepared loaf tin and bake for 1 hour or until
    a skewer inserted into the middle of the loaf comes out
    clean. Lightly cover with tinfoil halfway through cooking
    time to avoid the top browning too much.

5. For the syrup, mix sugar/honey and lemon/lime juice
    together. Remove loaf from oven, use a skewer to poke
    several holes all over the top, then pour over syrup while
    it is still warm in the tin. Allow syrup to soak in and loaf
    to cool slightly before removing from the tin. Serve warm
    or cold.

The loaf will keep in the fridge (in an airtight container) for
up to 5 days or can be frozen.

GF | DF | V

Energy	205kcal (858kJ)
Protein	6.1g
Carbohydrate	24.5g (21.0g sugars)
Fat	9.9g (1.0g sat fat)

FROZEN CHOCOLATE GRAPES.

Makes:	4 portions
Prep time:	5–10 minutes + at least 8 hours freezing time

400g bunch seedless grapes
(with stalk still attached)
50g good-quality dark
(e.g. 70% cocoa) chocolate,
finely chopped
1 level teaspoon coconut oil

Frozen grapes are a favourite little sweet treat – they're a bit like candy! A whole bunch coated in chocolate looks cool, but feel free to drizzle a tray of individual frozen grapes with chocolate and they'll be easier to eat that way.

1. Wash grapes, then delicately pat the bunch dry with paper towels. Freeze for at least 8 hours or overnight.

2. Gently heat chocolate and coconut oil together either in a bowl in the microwave in 30-second bursts (stirring gently in between) or in a double boiler or glass bowl set above a pot of barely simmering water.

3. Hold grape bunch by its stem above the bowl of melted chocolate and dip into chocolate. Use a spoon to pour/drizzle melted chocolate all over the grapes.

4. Alternatively, freeze individual (picked) grapes in a large dish lined with baking paper, then drizzle chocolate all over grapes (one way, and then the other way).

5. Return grapes to freezer for at least 15 minutes to allow the chocolate to harden.

V	GF	DF (use DF chocolate)		

Energy	100kcal (417kJ)
Protein	1.6g
Carbohydrate	9.1g (8.5g sugars)
Fat	6.2g (4.0g sat fat)

Makes:	4 portions
Prep time:	15 minutes

1½ cups frozen berries, thawed
2 tablespoons runny honey or
    maple syrup
⅔ cup cream
¾ teaspoon vanilla bean paste
    (or seeds from 1 vanilla
    bean pod)
1¼ cup unsweetened natural
    yoghurt or coconut yoghurt
2 cups freeze-dried fruit pieces
    (e.g. lychees, pineapple,
    feijoa), lightly crumbled

Freeze-dried fruit gives that sweet, crunchy texture that meringues give an Eton Mess, but without the copious amounts of sugar! You can find freeze-dried fruit (we use a brand called Fresh As) at gourmet food stores. Instead of berries, you could also chop up canned apricots or black doris plums.

1. Combine the berries with the honey/maple syrup in a bowl and mix well until the berries start to break up a little and release their juices.
2. Whisk cream in a large bowl until soft peaks form, add the vanilla paste and whisk a little more until medium peaks form. Fold through yoghurt.
3. Gently fold the juicy berries into the yoghurt cream.
4. To assemble, take 4 serving glasses and place a few tablespoons of crumbled freeze-dried fruit into each, layer with ⅓–½ cup yoghurt cream, another few tablespoons of freeze-dried fruit and a final layer of yoghurt cream. Garnish with any extra berries (fresh or frozen) and freeze-dried fruit.

Energy   254kcal (1062kJ)
Protein   5.4g
Carbohydrate   18.7g (16.9g sugars)
Fat   17.4g (10.5g sat fat)

GRILLED STONE FRUIT AND CUSTARD
WITH MACAROON TOPPING.

Makes:	4 portions
Prep time:	20 minutes
Cook time:	25 minutes

4 large ripe stone fruit (e.g.
   nectarines or peaches)
   or 8 small stone fruit
   (e.g. plums or apricots)
   or a combination
1 tablespoon honey

Macaroon topping
¾ cup desiccated coconut or
   coconut thread
1 free-range egg white
2 tablespoons honey
Good pinch of salt
2 tablespoons flaked almonds
¼ teaspoon vanilla extract
   or essence
Finely grated zest of ½ lemon

Vanilla custard
1½ level tablespoons
   custard powder
1 free-range egg yolk
1½ cups milk
½ teaspoon vanilla extract
   or essence
1½ tablespoons maple syrup

Fruit and custard is one of life's simple pleasures. We've taken it up a notch by adding a delicious coconut macaroon topping – simply delicious.

Preheat oven to 180°C.

1. Spread coconut over an oven tray in one even layer and toast in the oven for 3–4 minutes or until light golden. Transfer to a dish to cool.

2. Switch oven to grill. Pour 3 tablespoons water into a medium baking dish. Cut stone fruit in half (leave stones in) and place cut-side up in dish. Drizzle with honey. Grill for 10–15 minutes until soft and slightly caramelised on top.

3. While fruit grills, make macaroon topping. In a medium mixing bowl, beat egg white with an electric beater until soft peaks form, then add honey and salt and continue beating for a further few minutes until meringue is thick and glossy. Gently and briefly fold in cooled toasted coconut, almonds, vanilla and lemon zest (trying not to knock out any air) until evenly distributed.

4. Once cooked, remove fruit from oven and set aside to cool a little (they will be very, very hot). Change oven setting to bake at 180°C. When cool enough to handle, you can use a teaspoon or small knife to pop the stones out from the soft fruit flesh.

5. Dollop macaroon mixture over the top of fruit and return to oven to bake for 10–12 minutes until golden (watch it doesn't burn).

6. To make vanilla custard, in a small pot whisk custard powder, egg yolk and ¼ cup of the milk together until smooth. Whisk in remaining milk and bring to the boil on the stove top, then reduce heat and simmer for 2 minutes, whisking frequently, until thickened. Whisk in vanilla and maple syrup.

To serve, spoon custard into bowls and top with macaroon-topped grilled fruit.

GF	V	DF (use DF milk)

Energy	332kcal (1388kJ)
Protein	8.3g
Carbohydrate	34.4g (31.3g sugars)
Fat	17.0g (11.4g sat fat)

Makes:	6 portions
Prep time:	10 minutes
Cook time:	20–25 minutes + at least 1 hour freezing time

200g soft ricotta cheese
100g reduced-fat cream cheese, softened
1 free-range egg
2 tablespoons lime or lemon juice
Zest of 1 lime or ½ lemon
1 teaspoon vanilla extract or essence
⅓ cup honey
2 teaspoons GF flour
Pulp of 2 passionfruit

To serve
Pulp of 1 passionfruit (optional)
¼ cup muesli or granola (e.g. Chewy No-Grainola (see page 54) or Apple and Apricot Puff Muesli (page 40)

This recipe takes all of 10 minutes to prepare, before being baked in the oven. It's got the lovely creamy richness of a baked cheesecake, but with less than half the calories.

Preheat oven to 150°C. Line an 18cm square or similar size rectangular tin/dish with baking paper.

1. In a large mixing bowl, use an electric beater to beat ricotta, cream cheese, egg, lime/lemon juice and zest, vanilla and honey together until smooth. Briefly beat in flour until incorporated. Gently fold through passionfruit pulp.

2. Spoon mixture into prepared tin/dish and bake for 20–25 minutes or until cheesecake is just set with a slight wobble in the middle. Place in the freezer for at least 1 hour or in the fridge for at least 2–3 hours until cold and just firm enough to cut.

3. To serve, cut cheesecake into 6 even portions. Drizzle with a little more passionfruit pulp and sprinkle with muesli or granola.

GF | V

Energy	200kcal (834kJ)
Protein	7.0g
Carbohydrate	21.4g (20.3g sugars)
Fat	9.2g (4.9g sat fat)

UPSIDE-DOWN PLUM BABY CAKES WITH SWEET SPICE AND ORANGE.

Makes:	12 portions
Prep time:	20 minutes
Cook time:	15 minutes

1 tablespoon butter or coconut
   oil, melted
2 tablespoons muscavado,
   coconut or brown sugar
6 small plums, stones removed
   and each cut into 8 small
   wedges
50g butter or coconut oil,
   softened
⅓ cup honey
3 free-range eggs (at room
   temperature)
¾ cup GF or plain flour
1½ teaspoons baking powder
½ cup ground almonds
½ teaspoon ground cardamom
½ teaspoon ground cinnamon
1 tablespoon orange zest plus
   2 tablespoons orange juice

To serve
½ cup unsweetened natural
   yoghurt or coconut yoghurt

This recipe can also be made as one whole cake, if you prefer – use a 21cm round spring-form cake tin (lined with baking paper) and bake for 30 minutes.

Preheat oven to 180°C. Lightly grease a 12-hole medium muffin tin with butter or coconut oil.

1. Combine melted butter/coconut oil and sugar and divide between each muffin tin hole, then add 3–4 plum slices to each.

2. In a large mixing bowl, beat softened butter/coconut oil and honey together well with a wooden spoon, then add eggs, one at a time, beating well after each addition. Note that the mixture may look a bit curdled or split at this stage, and it's nothing to worry about as it will come back together when you mix in the dry ingredients.

3. Sift in flour and baking powder and fold in with the ground almonds, spices, orange zest and juice. Spoon the cake batter evenly over the plums and bake for about 15 minutes or until puffed and golden.

4. Allow to rest for 10 minutes then carefully invert the muffin tin onto a flat tray to release the little cakes. Spoon over any remaining plum juices from the muffin tin. Serve with yoghurt.

V
GF (use GF flour)
DF (use coconut oil and yoghurt)

Energy	157kcal (658kJ)
Protein	3.8g
Carbohydrate	18.3g (11.8g sugars)
Fat	7.8g (3.3g sat fat)

REAL FRUIT
ICE CREAMS.

We love real fruit ice cream – such a delicious,
refreshing treat that's good for you!

Makes:	4 portions
Prep time:	5 minutes

500g frozen boysenberries
¼ cup cream or coconut cream
¼ cup unsweetened natural
    yoghurt or coconut yoghurt
1–2 tablespoons apple syrup or
    maple syrup (optional)

1. Place all ingredients in a food processor and blitz until smooth, scraping down the sides a few times during blending to make sure everything is incorporated.
2. Taste the ice cream, and if you would like it a little sweeter, add the apple syrup or maple syrup and blitz to incorporate it. Serve ice cream immediately, or scoop into a container and return to the freezer until ready to serve (bring out to thaw on bench for 10 minutes first). Best eaten within 4 hours of making.

GF | V | DF (use coconut cream and yoghurt)

Energy	136kcal (570kJ)
Protein	3.0g
Carbohydrate	13g (12.9g sugars)
Fat	7.1g (4.1g sat fat)

Makes:	4 portions
Prep time:	5 minutes

3 cups frozen chopped
   mango pieces
1 frozen peeled and chopped
   ripe banana
Juice of 2 limes
Finely grated zest of 1 lime
¾ cup coconut yoghurt
2 teaspoons honey

1. Place all ingredients in a food processor and blitz until smooth, scraping down the sides a few times during blending to make sure everything is incorporated.
2. Either serve immediately, or transfer to a container and freeze until ready to serve (bring out to thaw on bench for 10 minutes first). Best eaten within 4 hours of making.

DF	GF	V

Energy	170kcal (709kJ)
Protein	2.0g
Carbohydrate	20.8g (19.1g sugars)
Fat	8.2g (3.4g sat fat)

Makes:	6 portions
Prep time:	15 minutes
Cook time:	5 minutes

Salted caramel date sauce
4–5 pitted medjool dates, chopped
½ cup water
Pinch of ground cinnamon
1 tablespoon maple syrup
¼ cup cream or coconut cream
Good pinch of salt

3 large frozen peeled and
   chopped ripe bananas
1½ cups natural unsweetened
   yoghurt or coconut yoghurt
1 teaspoon vanilla bean paste
   (or seeds of 1 vanilla bean pod)
2 tablespoons maple syrup
¼ cup toasted pecans, finely
   chopped

1. To make the salted caramel date sauce, boil dates and water together in a small pot for 1–2 minutes, stirring and breaking dates up with a spoon, until mushy. Transfer to a blender along with cinnamon, maple syrup, cream/coconut cream and salt, and blend until smooth. Set aside.

2. Place frozen bananas, yoghurt, vanilla and maple syrup in a food processor and blitz until smooth and creamy, scraping down the sides a few times during blending to make sure everything is incorporated. Transfer to a container, mix in half the pecans, and drizzle the top with the date caramel sauce. Sprinkle with remaining pecans, cover and freeze until ready to serve (bring out to thaw on bench for 10 minutes first). Best eaten within 4 hours of making.

Makes:	12 portions
Prep time:	15 minutes + at least 2 hours freezer time

½ cup coconut oil
¼ cup maple syrup
½ cup dark cocoa or cacao powder
1 teaspoon vanilla extract or essence
Pinch of flaky sea salt
⅓ cup dried fruit (e.g. raisins, sultanas, chopped dried apricots, cranberries or cherries)
⅓ cup chopped nuts (e.g. pistachios, almonds, hazelnuts)

Sometimes you just feel like a little piece of chocolate – here's the answer!

Line a baking or slice tin with baking paper and make sure there is enough space in the freezer for it to be stored flat.

1. Melt coconut oil in a small pot on low heat or in a medium bowl in the microwave. Allow coconut oil to cool.

2. Once cooled, whisk in maple syrup, cocoa/cacao powder, vanilla and salt until smooth.

3. Spoon mixture into lined tin and let it spread out (with the help of a spatula if needed) so that it is about 0.5cm thick. Sprinkle with fruit and nuts. Place in freezer, on a flat surface, for at least 2 hours or until frozen solid, then remove and cut into 12 squares or break into bark (in roughly equal-sized portions). Store in freezer in an airtight container for 6–8 weeks.

DF | GF | V

Energy	163kcal (681kJ)
Protein	2.2g
Carbohydrate	8.0g (7.0g sugars)
Fat	13.3g (9g sat fat)

Makes:	4 portions
Prep time:	10 minutes + 4–8 hours fridge time (for labne)
Cook time:	20 minutes

Labne

1½ cups unsweetened natural yoghurt or coconut yoghurt
¾ teaspoon vanilla bean paste (or seeds of 1 vanilla bean pod)
Finely grated zest of ½ orange
¼ teaspoon ground cinnamon
1–1½ tablespoons honey

Roast figs

8 large plump, ripe figs (if figs are small, you may want to use 12)
3 tablespoons honey
Leaves of 1–2 sprigs rosemary
Zest of 1 lemon
Juice of 1 orange

Make the labne (a thickened yoghurt flavoured with honey and orange) for this dessert at least 4 hours ahead of when you want to serve it. Pears or stone fruit would also be lovely cooked and served this way. If using pears, quarter lengthways and feel free to leave the core and stem attached for a more natural look. For stone fruit, simply cut in half – you can remove the stones after they're cooked, when it's much easier to do so.

1. To make the labne, place yoghurt in a muslin cloth or clean tea towel lining a sieve and set over a large bowl. Cover with a plate or cling film and place in the fridge for 4–8 hours, or overnight, until much of the whey has drained into the bowl and the yoghurt left behind is very thick. Transfer thick yoghurt to a bowl and mix with vanilla, orange zest, cinnamon and honey.

2. When ready to roast figs, preheat oven to 200°C. Cut figs in half lengthways. Place in a baking dish, drizzle with honey, scatter over rosemary leaves and lemon zest and squeeze over orange juice.

3. Roast for 10 minutes or until figs are soft and juicy, then switch to grill and continue to cook for about a further 8 minutes. Baste with the syrup in the dish and allow figs to cool.

Serve 4 fig halves per person, with a dollop of labne and a drizzle of syrup from the dish.

GF	V	DF (use coconut yoghurt)		

Energy	204kcal (851kJ)
Protein	5.7g
Carbohydrate	40.5g (39.4g sugars)
Fat	0.9g (0.3g sat fat)

Makes:	16 portions
	(1 cookie per portion)
Prep time:	20 minutes
Cook time:	30 minutes

¼ cup melted coconut oil
    or butter
⅓ cup muscavado, coconut or
    brown sugar
1 teaspoon vanilla extract or
    essence
1 free-range egg
½ cup GF or plain flour
1½ tablespoons good-quality
    dark cocoa or cacao powder
1 cup desiccated coconut
    plus 1–2 teaspoons extra
    for sprinkling
50g good-quality dark
    (e.g. 70% cocoa) chocolate,
    finely chopped

Icing
50g good-quality dark
    (e.g. 70% cocoa) chocolate,
    chopped
1 teaspoon coconut oil or butter
1 teaspoon maple syrup

Oh yes, bet you didn't think you'd find chocolate cookies in this cookbook! They're a chocolate-and-coconut-lover's dream, but with only 140 calories per cookie!

Preheat the oven to 180°C and line a large oven tray with baking paper.

1. In a large mixing bowl, whisk melted coconut oil/butter, sugar, vanilla and egg together until well combined.

2. Sift in flour and cocoa/cacao, and add coconut and chocolate. Stir gently until mixture is just combined.

3. Roll tablespoons of mixture into walnut-sized balls and place on lined tray, leaving space between each one. Flatten each cookie slightly with a fork.

4. Bake for 12–15 minutes. Allow to cool for a few minutes before transferring to a cooling rack to cool completely before icing.

5. To make icing, melt chocolate in a small pot with coconut oil/butter and maple syrup, stirring together well. Allow to cool slightly. Use a knife to ice the top of each cookie (or if icing is runny, lightly dip top of each cookie) and place back on cooling rack. Sprinkle with extra coconut. Allow to cool completely before storing in an airtight container for up to 2 weeks, or freeze in a resealable bag for up to a couple of months.

V
GF (use GF flour)
DF (use coconut oil and DF chocolate)

Energy	144kcal (604kJ)
Protein	1.8g
Carbohydrate	9.8g (5.6g sugars)
Fat	10.8g (8.4g sat fat)

Makes:	1 portion (but can be easily doubled, tripled or quadrupled)
Prep time:	5 minutes
Cook time:	45–60 seconds

1½ tablespoons GF or plain flour
1 tablespoon dark cocoa or cacao powder
⅛ teaspoon baking powder
Pinch of salt
2 teaspoons coconut oil or butter
1 tablespoon maple syrup
1 tablespoon chopped dark (e.g. 70% cocoa) chocolate (10g or 2 squares)
2 tablespoons milk

If the mood for a bit of chocolate pudding suddenly strikes you, here's the perfect solution – a super quick chocolate pud you can whip up in less than 5 minutes! What a treat!

1. Sift flour, cocoa, baking powder and salt into a medium bowl.

2. In a small bowl, melt coconut oil/butter, maple syrup and chocolate together (for 20–30 seconds in the microwave) and stir until smooth. Stir in milk.

3. Add chocolate mixture to flour mixture and mix with a spoon until just combined, but be careful not to overmix.

4. Spoon into a medium ramekin or mug and microwave for 45–60 seconds, or until puffed and still slightly gooey.

Serve immediately, by itself, or with a splash of milk or small dollop of yoghurt.

Tip: If you don't have a microwave, bake mug cake in a 180°C oven for 12–14 minutes.

V	GF	DF (use coconut oil, DF chocolate and DF milk)		
			Energy	296kcal (1236kJ)
			Protein	4.5g
			Carbohydrate	25.4g (15.7g sugars)
			Fat	19.4g (15g sat fat)

'Woahzers', creating this book has been a big undertaking, and it simply wouldn't have made it across the line without the help of a stellar line-up of people that I'm very fortunate to know, work with and call my buddies. You guys deserve much, much more than thanks in a paragraph (so we'll catch up for celebration drinks soon!), but here goes....

'Toddy' aka Todd Eyre, for the gorgeous photography, your patience and being a great mate and surf buddy. Amanda Gaskin and Tim Donaldson for designing such a beautiful book – you guys outdo yourselves every time, we simply LOVE your work and you are such fun people too. Jo Wilcox for stepping in to help with some of the food styling and beautiful attention to detail, and Natalie for use of your props.

Tracey Borgfeldt – big thanks for being so patient with me and getting this project over the line in time once again! And Kent Bowyer-Sidwell for instilling confidence and making the whole process seamless. Hayley Dodd for jumping in last minute to help out with some testing, and Siana Clifford and Jane Hingston for the great editing once again.

The core Fresh Start Bag team – Craig 'Coriander' Rodger, Emma 'Edamame' Wylie, Polly 'Pomegranate' Brodie and Anton 'Allspice' Leyland – who've been pivotal in the creation of the Fresh Start Bag which has helped our thousands of customers eat delicious, nutritious food and crush their weight-loss goals! Thanks also to Sarah 'Strawberry' Moller, Kellie 'Kingfish' Douglas, Ellie 'Honey' Hackshaw, Matt 'Pepper' Paul and Louise 'Chorizo' Cunningham from the marketing team for your input. Extra thanks and shout-out to Emma for being a super star with the nutrition analyses (I appreciate it so much as I know how big a job it is!), and Ellie for getting in your togs and going swimming with me!

Cecilia 'Chilli' and James 'Ravioli' Robinson – thank you for the vision and growing Fresh Start to what it's become... as Carlos would say, 'Boom!'

Better not forget my wonderful husband Carlos and son Bodhi too! You have no idea how much they have to put up while I'm creating a book!

Last, but not least, a big 'high five!' and thank you to all of our awesome Fresh Start Bag customers and supporters of the original Fresh Start Cookbook who've been along the journey, shared their kick-ass success stories, and given me great feedback, love and encouragement. You have no idea how much it means to me – I'm indebted to you for all the smiles, warm-fuzzies and satisfaction I get from doing what I love. THANK YOU.

Big hugs, love and gratitude,

nadia x

Text © Nude Food Inc, 2018
Photographs © Todd Eyre, 2018
Typographical design © Nude Food Inc, 2018
Book design: Seachange Studio, Auckland

Published in 2018 by Nude Food Inc,
Auckland, New Zealand

www.nadialim.com www.myfoodbag.co.nz

ISBN 978-0-473-44528-7

Prepress and Book Production – Benefitz,
New Zealand

Printed in China